LION'S HEAD, FOUR HAPPINESS

Xiaomei Martell was born in 1964 in Inner Mongolia, one of China's most remote regions, and spent her formative years there during the Cultural Revolution. After winning a coveted university place at the age of fifteen, she went to study English and then art in Beijing, where she also worked after graduation, teaching English, acting as a travel guide and working for art galleries. She came to England in the late 1980s to pursue her studies and has lived in England ever since.

XIAOMEI MARTELL

Lion's Head, Four Happiness

A Little Sister's Story of Growing up in China

VINTAGE BOOKS
London

Published by Vintage 2009

4 6 8 10 9 7 5 3

Copyright © Xiaomei Martell 2009

First published in Great Britain in 2009 by

Vintage
Random House, 20 Vauxhall Bridge Road,
London SW1V 2SA

www.vintage-books.co.uk

Addresses for companies within The Random House Group Limited can be
found at: www.randomhouse.co.uk/offices.htm

The Random House Group Limited Reg. No. 954009

A CIP catalogue record for this book
is available from the British Library

ISBN 9780099532095

The Random House Group Limited supports The Forest Stewardship Council
(FSC), the leading international forest certification organisation.
All our titles that are printed on Greenpeace approved FSC certified paper
carry the FSC logo. Our paper procurement policy can be found at
www.rbooks.co.uk/environment

Printed and bound in Great Britain by
CPI Cox & Wyman, Reading RG1 8EX

To my mother

Contents

I

Food to Celebrate

The king prawns are almost too good for sweet and sour. Freshly caught in the Yellow Sea that morning, they sit beautifully on an equally beautiful bone-china plate. Amid the symphony of chopping, chatting and the clattering of pans and woks comes the scent of fresh coriander, toasted chilli and a mixture of ginger, spring onion and garlic. The star anise wafts through from a pot of mouth-watering tender beef from the cattle bred on the lush steppes of Inner Mongolia.

This is one of the very few birthday celebrations we have had for my mother, soon to be 80. In fact, we have only started to celebrate her birthday recently. My lasting memory of a birthday celebration when my sisters and I were young, was for the birthday girl to have two eggs and the other siblings to have one each. In Meiling's case, as her birthday falls in July, she was able to have two juicy peaches, instead of eggs. Meiling, a born fruit lover, ate her peaches avidly but was very careful not to waste any. Her bright, almond-shaped eyes sometimes betrayed a little guilt as she spotted me watching her eating her second peach. 'Have a small bite,' she would offer, holding her peach close to my mouth with an air of indulgence from an elder sibling who would proudly tell everybody she was not just one year older, but one and a half years older than me. Embarrassed but very tempted, I would take a small bite, just a little in front of her two fingers that were holding the peach tight, the unspoken line that I should not pass. My mother often skipped the eggs and the peaches, in the same way that she skipped her birthday. Not that she was not fond of such treats – for eggs and peaches were treats when I was young – nor that she could not bear the thought of her advancing years, she simply wanted to save the eggs and peaches for us, her brood of four daughters.

Having four daughters is not particularly something my parents should have had a reason to celebrate, not where we were, a Chinese city on the borders of the Mongolian steppes. As a child, I liked the sound of Huhehot, the name of our city, which meant 'Green Town' in Mongolian. It sounded particularly alluring when Mongolians pronounced it in their resonant voices, and I occasionally imitated the Mongolians, only to be teased by my sisters. Sometimes I used to feel that it was a little unfair when adults referred to our city, the capital city of Inner Mongolia, as a small city, almost with the implication that it was remote and less developed than other Chinese cities or even somewhat backward.

Unlike boys, girls cannot pass on the family name. 'Boys are yours, girls are somebody else's,' Madam Guan, our next-door neighbour, lamented when her eldest daughter got married and moved in with her in-laws. This was what people did at that time. As a child, I could not understand why Madam Guan was not more pleased when her daughter left. After all, their cramped mid-terrace house, a three-room one-storey house similar to ours, would be a little less crowded with only seven remaining children. 'But what do you know, you are only a young girl, little No. 4,' a thin and stern-looking Madam Guan sighed, her tobacco-stained front teeth seeming to protrude more than ever, emphasising her last word. I rolled my eyes at her in frustration, to the amusement of her eighth child, or No. 8. Apart from anything else, I hated being referred to in such a way, a local custom commonly used by rather uneducated people. 'Her name means Little Sister,' Meiling would often take the opportunity to lecture Madam Guan on my name. Madam Guan was about as literate as an average ten-year-old, but that doesn't mean she was not smart – she was pretty streetwise. In spite of her fierce appearance and straight talking, Mother said that she was really quite kind. She often had a chat with my mother over the fence under our apricot tree which bore small, sharp fruits. Having fruits from our tree was delightful, though it became a centre of attention for a group of local boys who had broken many branches stealing our fruit before it even had a chance to become ripe. My parents loved trees, particularly my mother, who often talked, with a touch of nostalgia, about the wisteria and the lilac tree in the garden of the courtyard house she grew up in. 'A wasted horticultural talent,' I heard Madam Guan saying on more than one occasion when she saw my mother explaining to us the shapes of plant leaves or taking us to flower shows in the parks. My parents also planted a poplar tree and a lilac tree in our front garden, or the courtyard as we sometimes grandly called it.

Being a girl, I should do less talking and more cooking, Madam Guan told me. At least, I should start to learn. It was laughable for a girl not to be able to cook, not to mention the prospect of not turning out to be a good wife. But there was little to cook with because of the rationing. 'Even the best housewife struggles to cook without rice,' Meiling came to my defence by repeating an old saying she had picked up somewhere, probably from Madam Guan herself.

I was born into rationing. Rationing was introduced across China after three difficult years triggered by natural disasters and poor economic planning in the late 1950s and early 60s. In spite of the rationing, my parents celebrated my arrival on the shortest day in 1964 with *jiaozi*, bite-sized dumplings and a festival food often linked to the Chinese New Year. 'Little sister, little sister, dumplings will give you perfect ears,' five-year-old Yan hopped around me, with the excitement of a somewhat boisterous elder sister. She constantly touched my small nose, which still bore a trace of the snowflakes that had fallen on me when my father picked my mother and me up earlier from the hospital in a pedicab, quite a luxury in our city at that time. She was chanting a popular rhyme which, I later learnt, was about the local custom of eating dumplings on the shortest day of the year, said to protect the ears from freezing in the cold weather ahead. Thinking about it now, I am not certain whether my parents were true followers of such customs, but I am pretty sure that they would only be too pleased that the dumplings, a delicious treat, killed two birds with one stone.

I knew how to say the word rationing long before I knew the meaning of it. I remember as a four-year-old holding on to the edge of a basket of apples, brought over by somebody keen to establish a favour with my father who was a senior official in the railway bureau, one of the largest employers in the city. It was a nice autumn day, with the sun shining high in the bright blue sky and a few beautiful pieces of white cloud floating about. I was looking at those apples longingly, they were small green apples tainted with a blush of red, patriotically branded as Country Pride. The guest's conversation with my father seemed to meander, which is what one did to establish connections, or *guanxi*. *Guanxi* was terribly useful, not least because it brought us delicious fruits and other foods which were in limited supply. My father was a mild and indulgent man who rarely told me off. But I knew the rules, and it was poor form to eat the apples before the guest left. I moved the basket lid up and down, secretly hoping that this would distract them from their conversation and that the guest would soon leave, so that I could have one of the crunchy apples. But my scheme was not working, and I started counting, miserably, the movement of the long hand on the blue clock on my father's prized walnut desk. The clock seemed to conspire against me, with its long hand moving

4

really slowly. All I could do, then, it seemed, was to look at the apples and be contented with the thought that the apple would be mine to eat soon. This was a magical thought, and mouth-wateringly satisfying.

Food always seemed to be in short supply in our Mongolian city. The long and harsh winters did nothing to help with the local produce. 'Potatoes, mutton and sheepskin are our three treasures' was a playground rhyme. Even with the potatoes, which seemed to be plentiful, we had to have the rejects. Mr Guan, Madam Guan's husband, was a supervisor on a farm affili-ated to the railway bureau, and one day I heard him saying that the biggest and the best potatoes went to the polar bears, as he called the Soviets. I didn't really understand what he was talking about, except that he sounded angry when talking about the Russians. 'Behave yourself,' Madam Guan told her husband, as she saw Meng Hong, my sister Yan's friend walking past. Meng Hong, a striking brown-eyed beauty with high cheekbones which she must have inherited from her Russian grandmother, was the envy of the girls in our neighbourhood. 'That's when the Russians were our friends,' Mr Guan, who was a little henpecked, muttered. He was probably referring to Meng Hong's grand-mother having married a Chinese man.

Food did not travel much then, and there was not a lot of choice in our city even in summer. We had a short season for tomatoes and other fresh fruit and vegetables. When Yan was a teenager, she was particularly fond of hanging out with her friends from the school's Revolutionary Propaganda Troupe, the school's music and drama group. She took it upon herself to buy fresh and sometimes not-so-fresh vegetables for us during the summer holidays. With some of her musical friends, knocking on our door at the crack of dawn, she would some-times leave at five in the morning to join the long queues, even

5

though the stalls would not open till eight o'clock. 'I'll get you some big juicy tomatoes today,' she liked to boast to Meiling and me. With rationing, each person in the queue was limited to buying a certain amount of fresh produce, say 1 kilogram of tomatoes, 1/2 kilo of cucumbers and 1 kilo of spinach or whatever greens were available. By being at the front of the queue, she thought she would automatically get at least a few juicy tomatoes, even if the shop assistants put them on to the scales randomly, as claimed; and by the law of averages, she should have. But Yan was not so lucky, and more often than not she would end up with poor tomatoes, either small and green, or over-ripe. 'Why do all the juicy ones have to disappear just before my turn to buy?' she complained one day after she told us how she often counted the tomatoes in the pile behind the counter and how she prayed that the shop assistants would not reserve the remaining tomatoes for their friends and contacts.

Small or over-ripe, tomatoes are still one of our favourite summer foods, and a key ingredient in a much-loved dish that my mother cooked. Breaking the eggs into a bowl, she would add a third of a teaspoonful of salt before beating the eggs thoroughly with a pair of bamboo chopsticks. To increase the volume, she would add a tablespoon of cold water to the mixture while beating, before chopping three tomatoes into quarters, then each piece again into halves. Preparation done, she would heat the wok and then put in half a tablespoon of vegetable oil until the oil was very hot. The magical moment for me, when I was young, was when I heard the sizzling sound as she poured the egg mixture into the hot oil. The sound, the sensation and the anticipation were all delicious. The hot oil always did the trick by making the egg mixture expand into a golden yellow 'pancake'. A moment later, she would shake the wok a little before turning the eggs over, often by throwing them into the air. It was fascinating to see how she always managed to make the lightly fried eggs land back in the wok, a skill we found very entertaining when we were small. Once the eggs were done, she would get them out on to one of our plates before cooking the tomatoes in a third of a tablespoon of vegetable oil, putting the tomatoes in only once the oil was hot. Then she would stir-fry them until the tomatoes became soft. The eggs, now chopped into bite-sized pieces, were transferred back into the wok, stirred, and mixed with the tomatoes, before she added a teaspoon of soy sauce, a third of a teaspoonful of salt and a couple of teaspoonfuls of sugar together with a tablespoon of boiled water. Then stir for a couple of minutes, and a tasty dish is born. Fried eggs and tomatoes is such a simple dish, but it has always been a much-loved dish in our family, and is undoubtedly one of the most popular dishes in China.

My mother grew up in a beautiful seaside town, not far from the foot of the Great Wall, and she loves seafood. Seafood was a great treat for us, and in our Mongolian city in the 1960s it was almost impossible to get fresh sea fish. Very occasionally we could get carp from the Yellow River, which flows through Inner Mongolia, and that was the freshest fish we had. I still remember the first time that I had the Yellow River carp. Freshly steamed and sprinkled with finely chopped spring onion, ginger, garlic and coriander, the melting, succulent fish looked seductive on my parents' best oval plate. To be honest, I cannot be certain how many times we actually had fresh carp from the Yellow River. Sometimes, I wondered whether it was my fantasy at work. Fantasy can be a great thing. My mother told me a story one day when I was longing for a banana, which was a rarity in our city at the time. One swelteringly hot summer's day, my mother recounted, an army troop, hot and thirsty, became slower and slower as it marched towards its enemy.

The sky was cloudless, there was no breeze and no water nearby for the troop or its horses. Morale was low and the commander-in-chief grew worried. Then, suddenly something came to him. He rode to the front. 'Men, there is an orchard of plum trees just the other side of the mountain, big juicy plums,' he announced cheerfully. The very thought of the fruit falling into their mouths got the troops going and their thirst seemed to be quenched. They followed him, galloping in the direction of the enemy. This was something I could easily relate to at the time of the food shortages!

Fried cuttlefish was our Sunday treat. A friend of my mother tipped her off about a place where she could occasionally buy small cuttlefish and other not-so-good-quality seafood rejected by wholesalers. Mongolian people are, generally speaking, not very fond of seafood, and that was why, I was told, there were quite a few sufferers of hypothyroidism because of a deficiency of iodine in their diet. Because of the lack of interest in seafood in our city, my mother seemed to be able to get something most weekends. On Sunday mornings, my mother would get up really early to prepare the cuttlefish. She often sat on a small red wooden stool my father had bought from the south and usually under the lilac tree in our front garden, even when it was quite cold outside. She would wash the fish in one enamel bowl, and then, with a small knife and scissors, slowly and carefully remove the skin, and then the ink, in another enamel bowl filled with water before she transferred it to another container. It is a difficult task to remove the ink thoroughly and sometimes it is a messy job. On more than one occasion, my mother's apron was covered with spots of ink that had come out of the eyes of the cuttlefish. My mother had amazing patience and was keen not to waste anything. After what seemed to be hours of preparation, she would cut the fish into thin strips before blanching it in the boiling water. A quick stir-fry with finely shredded ginger and spring onions, a splash of vinegar and rice wine, and the cooked cuttlefish smelt like a feast. It was normally accompanied by the scent of steamed white rice, also a treat for us. Aubergine, if in season, was also a favoured accompaniment to the steamed rice. Usually cut into strips, the aubergine was fried in vegetable oil, with one roughly chopped tomato and a few cloves of garlic. Carefully dividing the cuttlefish into portions, with my parents always having the smaller portions, my mother would serve the fish on top of our rice in our best bowls brought out for the occasion. As the youngest in the family, I was often indulged and allowed to take my pick first. This was soon followed by the sound of delicious eating, with the inevitable occasional slurping. In children, slurping was quite often smiled upon as a sign of real enjoyment of food.

My mother was very happy if we helped with the cooking, but equally happy if we didn't help. 'You give those girls too easy a time,' Madam Guan would sometimes say about our rather liberal household. My mother always smiled when Madam Guan volunteered her thoughts. But it was not only her thoughts she volunteered; sometimes she would offer her expertise as well.

Madam Guan was good at pickled cabbage and she seemed to have identified a promising chef in my eldest sister Jing. Although Jing is only eight years older than me, as a child, I often thought that she was really grown-up and sophisticated. Jing was a quiet teenager who seemed to have a knack for cooking from an early age. The first steamed bread Jing made, when she was 12, was hailed as outstanding by Madam Guan, a very high accolade indeed from a highly critical but also very competent cook. My parents bought an oval urn for pickling one autumn day. Glazed in black with a light brown edge, the half-metre tall urn looked elegant next to the big water urn that we also had. Madam Guan was keen to teach Jing the art of pickling. But she insisted that the rest of us, though not so promising at cooking, had to learn as well. Having gathered all us girls together, including four of her own, she showed us the secrets of pickling. First, choose the cabbage with firmness in the middle, get rid of any rotten leaves, then wash the vegetables and leave them to drain in a large colander or on a big wooden chopping board. In the meantime, clean the urn thoroughly and then rinse it. Once the urn is clean, put in a small amount of cold water, and carefully layer the cabbage in the urn. Sprinkle some salt between the layers, then fill the urn, almost to the brim, with salt water. Finally, taking a good-sized piece of rock that had been washed earlier in the day, Madam Guan placed it on top of the vegetables, to stop them floating, before putting the wooden lid on the urn. Pickled cabbage is a traditional Manchurian dish and Madam Guan, born in Manchuria, said that her recipe had been handed down through the generations. It was important to get every step right, simple as it looked, she insisted.

Late autumn in our city often came with heavy rain which ushered in the start of the cold weather, with mosquitoes desperately catching a few final victims before they went into hibernation. Late autumn was also a time for pickled cabbage. On every street corner you would see piles and piles of Chinese long-leaf cabbages, stacked up like leafy sculptures. Our cellar, a two-metre deep, well-like structure with two wings at the bottom, dug in the garden, was already being filled with Chinese cabbage, our only leafy vegetable for the winter. The youngest of the Guan children – naughty No. 8 as his mother called him – was severely scolded by her when he was found trying to dig a tunnel between their cellar and ours. The cellars were favourites with us children when we played hide-and-seek.

It was the eighth birthday of the Guans' eighth child. Guan Jie, or No. 8 as he was better known, was the fourth son and the youngest of the Guans. Since eight, and especially double eight, is a lucky number, a number to bring in fortune and wealth, and Madam Guan was a great believer in such things, the day called for a big celebration. What's more, it fell on the eve of the Moon Festival, an annual festival on the lunar calendar, and was therefore an opportunity for double celebration. The front room was crammed with four tables, with three on the floor and one on the *kang*, a brick bed. A group of old people sat on the coal-heated bed, drinking *baijiu*, a strong liquor, locally distilled, with a clear hue like gin but with a much stronger taste. Thinking about it, it is now almost laughable for me to have thought of those people as being so old, as they were probably only in their fifties or at most, sixties. Jing was in charge of the table where most of the children congregated. Like many children, I was fascinated by the copper pots with small chimneys on top. To my young eyes, each round pot, at the centre of every table, was shaped like a dome with a tower in the middle. It was particular fun to watch Mr Guan adding a couple of hot pieces of charcoal into the chimney of each pot. The chimney was an integral part of the stove chamber and of the pot, the size of a medium saucepan. The charcoal seemed to work wonders, and the soup in the pot on our table was soon bubbling merrily. Having carefully removed the lid, which had an elaborate handle on each side, Jing started to put into the soup some finely-cut potato slices, bean curd and rice noodles before adding some wafer-thin slices of beef, lamb and mutton.

There were also dishes piled with Chinese cabbage waiting to go in. Jing did all this with considerable skill, her every move avidly watched by a group of children, all waiting to tuck in to the scrumptious Mongolian Hot Pot. Between tasks, she had to fend off the greedy children, eager to dip into the hot pot for meat slices before they were ready. With many pretty little dishes of green, red and yellow sauces, a few children, too tempted by the delicious cooking smell and the sauces, started to dip their chopsticks into the pot and the sauces. A few screams followed – either somebody had his hand steamed, or the spicy sauce proved too hot for a youngster. That was soon replaced by the excitement of having the first cooked pieces from the pot and the competition to obtain the best pieces. We children were soon fighting for the pieces of meat, and in fact for everything in the pot. No. 8 was the head of the pack at our table. He, taking advantage of his birthday, managed to hog most of the delicacies in the pot. Slurping contentedly, he started a game of paper-scissors-stone. The winner would win the chance to dip in the pot before him. The competition started reasonably fairly, and ended in tears when No. 8 cheated a girl out of her chance to secure the last bit of beef. The tears only ended when Jing offered her mutton to the girl.

A neighbour, who had recently had a pig slaughtered, brought in the trotters and ears, still steaming from the stew. She gave one of the pig trotters, smelling of star anise, to Madam Guan's eldest daughter, who was expecting a baby. 'Have this, very nutritious,' she smiled before she offered the other trotter to a table of mostly women. 'Good for *yin*, and good for our skin,' she said. Chinese love food and love to link well-being to food. I knew from an early age that dates were good for blood, sesame good for hair and vinegar good for the complexion. The pig ears, thanks to the chopping skill of Jing, looked a picture on a china plate, finely shredded and drizzled with a mixture of vinegar, soy sauce and sesame oil and garnished with fresh coriander leaves.

We had fireworks to chase away the evil spirits, just as we would normally do before the start of the Chinese New Year. The fireworks came in all shapes and sizes, mostly in red wrappers, with some going off with really loud bangs and some going off with a vivid display of colour and motion. The Guans splashed out on the fireworks this time, as we were also celebrating the forthcoming arrival of their first grandchild. As a young girl, I always thought one of the attractions of having a big family was to have many reasons for celebration and much food to celebrate.

2

The River and the Ducklings

I don't talk about my father much. The truth is that he rarely features in my childhood memories. He was absent for most of my childhood for reasons I still find difficult to describe and the fact of the matter is that I remember little of him.

The very few memories I have of him are stowed away like old photographs. Whenever I stumble upon them, consciously or subconsciously, it seems that those faded yet precious snapshots always take me back to that river and our 'dry ducklings'.

Down a steep hill not far from our house, there was a river which my parents sometimes used as a short cut to the shops on the other side. My mother, who was quite athletic, would jump from stepping stone to stepping stone and manage to cross the river without getting wet at all. By the river was a small wood where local children congregated to play among the trees and over the dam that spanned the river. I was never good at running on the dam, unlike Meiling who was good with heights. I was frightened of looking down at the flowing water, but I liked the river though, and loved dipping my feet into it or wading across it, often getting my trousers or skirt wet. Our clothes were mostly cotton or corduroy; some of them were made by my mother, but most were bought by my father during his business trips to Shanghai. My father was good at choosing clothes and the clothes he bought used to attract admiration from our neighbours for their superior quality and style and simply for being made in Shanghai, renowned for quality and style. He seemed to be fond of corduroy, partly because clothes made of corduroy were more durable.

Zhuji was a boy a few years older than me and we used to play together on the riverbank. He lived in one of the dwellings rendered with yellow mud, next to a big farmyard. About a dozen families lived there, as a part of what was called the People's Commune. I didn't understand the set-up as such but was always intrigued by the space they had in their yard where they grew vegetables and raised their poultry. I particularly liked their well and its cast-iron manual pump. In fact, we sometimes used the well to get our drinking water when the communal tap in our residential area froze up. 'They are peasants,' people in our neighbourhood used to say of the families in the People's Commune, some snobbish people even implying at times that they were a little inferior. In fact, they were just agricultural people working under the system of a commune, a product of the planned economy prevailing in China at that time. 'We have a lot of ducklings,' Zhuji announced one day. Ducklings surely meant eggs . . . my young mind was working fast. Eggs were a luxury in short supply. Apart from using the very few monthly coupons to buy them from a shop across the river, my parents were always trying to get more, and used our millet to swap for eggs with local farmers. Although millet, part of our main staple, was also bought on a restrictive basis, we managed to have some to spare most months – an advantage of having girls with smaller appetites, as our neighbour Madam Guan quickly pointed out. The swapping was done clandestinely. If somebody told the local police, the farmers' eggs, often hidden in canvas tool-bags, would be confiscated and my parents would be severely reprimanded, because it was considered bourgeois to do such trading.

I told my parents about the ducklings, and persuaded my mother to visit Zhuji's parents. She brought back five ducklings, and my father busied himself building them a house under the lilac tree in our garden. With only scraps of material and few tools, he managed to build a brick house with a wooden door. Aware of the hungry foxes around the neighbourhood, he made sure that the door was secured with the help of a couple of bricks every evening.

Our ducklings grew fast. So far, so good. For the moment though, there was one problem – our ducklings did not like water. Convinced that he could eventually lure them into the river, my father got us all to help him take the ducklings to the river. Most Sundays, all six of us would form a circle, with my parents taking the lead, to escort the flock of five 'dry' ducklings in the direction of the river. It often had a promising start, with the ducklings quacking away and marching merrily across the road and then to the wood, where they became rather focused on catching and eating worms. As soon as the river was in sight, they started to turn back, but were often cornered by us and made to face the river. They then started quacking again, this time quite unhappily, as if to say 'Why are we here?' You could take the ducklings to the water but you certainly could not make them swim.

But we were not disappointed with the ducklings. Out of the five, three were female, which meant we should have a good supply of eggs. Even the two male ones were gaining weight steadily, as if to show us that they would provide a good supplement to our rationed meat supply. My parents were a little dismayed that they were not all female as they didn't relish the thought of having to kill any birds for food, and this was strongly supported by Meiling who had become rather attached to the ducklings. She said that she would rather live on millet, potatoes and Chinese cabbage than eat one of our own ducks. But the sensible thing for my parents to do was perhaps to kill one drake eventually. Apart from anything, the ducks were eating into our millet supply.

Our ducks left us one spring afternoon as a sandstorm blew over from the Gobi Desert. The sky turned yellow and the sand blew into our eyes as we desperately searched for the ducklings. We went through all the narrow lanes and to the riverbank, fighting with the howling wind, flying sand and decreased visibility. That is one aspect of the climate in our Mongolian city which I hated as a young girl. Long freezing winters as cold as below minus 30°C were bad enough, burdening me with unfashionable padded trousers and jacket for many months. As soon as the spring beckoned, I was keen to shed the layers of warm clothing, only to find that spring did not necessarily bring warm weather and, almost as if the weather designed to conspire against me, the sandstorms arrived almost as soon as the weather was ready for spring clothing. Like all the girls, I had long devised a fashion scheme in spite of the weather. One of my favourite accessories, out of a very limited collection, was a pink scarf. I can still feel the fine, thin and transparent gauze. On a fine spring day, I would wear it as a scarf in many different ways. On a windy day, I would wear it as a veil. I told Meiling that was my way of stopping sand from blowing into my eyes and mouth, but, before she had a chance to tease me, I had to admit that this was more a fashion statement than a practical solution, because we both knew that the thin scarf didn't have much chance of stopping any blowing sand.

Our ducks never returned. According to Madam Guan, she saw a couple of foxes in our neighbourhood that day. 'But your ducks might be lucky,' she said, taking a deep drag on her cigarette butt. She always seemed to make one cigarette last for ever, and had the skill of holding on to the very end of the cigarette while still managing to smoke without burning her fingers. As usual, she was quick to offer another explanation. She said the Ma family, the newly arrived neighbours, had probably taken them. 'They are even more short of meat than us, because they don't eat pork,' she paused, partly to have another draw on her cigarette butt, and partly to give us some food for thought. 'They are *Huis*,' she said, pleased with her knowledge that the Mas were Chinese Muslims. 'You should have a search in their court-yard.' My parents were not in favour of such prejudice against our new neighbours and had no intention of pursuing our search in this manner. Besides, we were more or less resigned to our loss. To comfort us, my mother got out a couple of *songhua* eggs, a treat that was normally reserved for special occasions or when we had visitors. *Songhua* eggs, or hundred-year-old eggs, as they were known, are duck eggs preserved in lime. Coated in thick grey lime mixed with straw, the eggs have a pungent flavour and leave a strong after-taste, along with an occasional burning sensation on the tongue. Prepared properly, *songhua* eggs could be a treat. Scrape off the mud from the egg shell, peel and then rinse the eggs, taking care not to break them at this stage. Slice the eggs on a chopping board, and then carefully put the slices into a dish. Add finely chopped fresh ginger, a splash of vinegar and the eggs are now ready to eat, either as a starter or an accompaniment to other dishes. *Songhua* eggs, a little like very mature and smelly Brie, are something of an acquired taste.

Spring was not all about sandstorms, and spring pancakes were something to look forward to. Chinese people have been making this simple but delicious food for centuries, to celebrate the arrival of the spring. Spring pancakes are thin pancakes with at least two easily separated layers inside, with each layer acting as a pocket to fill with various delicious vegetables, stir-fried beforehand. Celery, chives and bamboo shoots are popular vegetable fillings for the traditionalists who like to chew on their symbolic link to industriousness, eternity and prosperity. My sister Jing was particularly good at making spring pancakes, and from a young age she mastered the art of making dough, the most difficult and important part of pancake making. She would first bring some water to the boil. Pouring plain flour into a big enamel bowl, she would carefully make a well in the middle with her chopsticks. Then she would pour the boiled water, slightly cooled down, into the well, and mix. After that, she would start to knead with her hands, occasionally having to stop kneading, briefly, to give her hands a break from the heat of the dough, which was partly cooked by the hot water. She would continue kneading until the dough reached the right elastic consistency. For an even better consistency and texture, she would sometimes make another piece of dough with cold water and knead it immediately into the hot dough. 'Three smooth: hand, dough and surface, is what you should achieve with dough making,' she used to say proudly as she ran her surprisingly flour-free hand over the smooth surface of the dough, with the enamel bowl shining. Dough making over, she would put a piece of damp muslin over the dough for it to rest. An hour or so later, the dough was ready. This she would knead into a long sausage shape which she then cut into small pieces. Putting three pieces together with a few drops of vegetable oil in between to create three layers, she would then roll out a pancake, ready to go into a preheated pan for a quick fry. Jing often added some fried shredded pork into her vegetable fillings, and they were delicious. Pancakes are best eaten hot. My mother liked to add some plum sauce into hers, as if it was Peking duck. Spring pancakes were similar to those pancakes eaten with Peking duck – the loss of our ducklings, however, made that but a dream.

Chinese people love to tell you how Marco Polo took the

ancient art of Chinese noodle making to Italy where noodles became spaghetti or tagliatelle. Noodles come in many shapes and forms, and they can be boiled, steamed or fried. Fried ones, known as *chaomian*, are probably best known. Adding some stir-fried vegetables and a few king prawns to them makes a simple and tasty dish. I was particularly fond of the 'flour fish' my mother used to make. Mixing flour in a bowl and kneading the dough many times until it was semi-soft, flexible and smooth, she would tilt the bowl in the direction of a saucepan of boiling water, and then use the side of a bamboo chopstick to slice the dough into shapes of small fish. All these fish would fall directly into the boiling water, and she would take them out after about five minutes and rinse briefly with cold water before serving. Flour fish tasted good even with just a drizzle of vinegar, a few thinly cut cucumber sticks and a few pieces of finely chopped spring onion and a pinch of fresh coriander. I used to put a drop of hot chilli sauce on mine, and it tasted divine. My mother learnt to make this dish from Madam Jiao, another neighbour. In our city, neighbours liked to swap recipes. It was particularly useful during rationing when everybody was keen to get the most out of their limited supply of food. Madam Jiao, a smart lady from Taiyuan, was particularly good at making noodles and pasta. Taiyuan, a city in neighbouring Shanxi province, was famous for its noodle making and its vintage vinegar, which was a superior vinegar, beautifully aged and flavoursome. Vinegar is precious to Shanxi people and they use it on nearly every dish. There was a joke spread in our city, saying that during the Chinese civil war, many Shanxi soldiers chose to surrender rather than hand over their vinegar flasks. True to her roots, Madam Jiao did use a lot of vinegar in her cooking. That's why, some neighbours said, her complexion was smooth and pale, as vinegar was clearly good for one's skin. Pale skin was considered to be good, particularly for a girl, and was far superior to dark or sun-tanned skin. After all, only the peasants working in the paddy fields had skin roughened by the elements.

Madam Jiao was a private and sometimes elusive woman. She always looked immaculate, her clothes nicely pressed and hair done up neatly every day when she went to work on her well-cleaned bicycle. She worked in the logistics department of the railway bureau. She limped a little because of childhood polio, but she didn't let that detract from her otherwise upright posture. Her house was just as tidy, and she seemed to spend most of her free time cleaning it and tidying the front garden. Meiling and I used to watch her with amazement picking up the leaves as they blew over from our trees to her garden. Somewhat naughtily, we used to invent conversations, with Meiling acting as Madam Jiao complaining about mountains of leaves built up in her imaginary back garden (no family in our neighbourhood had a back garden). Autumn was the most entertaining time for us to watch. Her speed at leaf clearing was incredible, and often she would get her adopted daughter Yaya to help. Yaya liked to please and, looking back, I can see her now walking around with her big head over her small shoulders, her big wide eyes full of longing and perhaps some sadness. She was five years or so older than me, but I could not remember her going to school. She was a dwarf, abandoned by her real mother who could not cope with her both being a girl and being deformed. Her artist father, Madam Jiao's brother, pleaded for his sister to take on his daughter. Without children of her own, Madam Jiao eventually agreed to adopt Yaya. Yaya was not to disappoint, and she became pretty good at cooking from a young age. In addition to making metre-long noodles, she could produce a good stir-fry under the supervision of Mr Wang, Madam Jiao's amiable husband.

Noodles and pancakes were more of a treat, however, and on most days we had to have 'wire noodles'. Wire noodles are very much like spaghetti, but made from sweet cornflour and rather chewy. There was a wire noodle making factory in our neighbourhood. Every lunchtime, there would be a queue of people, each carrying a bowl of sweet corn flour. Lunch was sacrosanct and everybody in our city seemed to go home for their long lunch breaks. When it was your turn, a lady behind the counter would take your flour and weigh it. You could not just go and buy some wire noodles, because we were all on rationing, and every kilo of flour was bought with staple vouchers. Once the weighing was out of the way, the flour would be poured into a big wooden mixing vat next to a noodle machine. Your bowl would then join a queue of bowls at the other end of the machine. All you needed to do was to pay the equivalent of a few pence and wait. I used to watch with fascination how a piece of dough was squeezed into noodles within seconds. If I was really hungry, I would eat some freshly processed wire noodles on the way home, before they were cooked in the steamer. Wire noodles formed a large part of our diet.

One day, my father's colleagues sent him two bags of milk powder. He was unwell, but I didn't know how unwell. I guessed that his illness must be pretty serious, otherwise his colleagues would not have sent him such nutritious food that was so difficult to get. Even without our ducks, my father still liked to take us to the river; sometimes he would take the wooden bath tub he had bought in the south, to try to preserve the wood. The dry Mongolian weather did the tub no favours and the solid wooden pieces gradually became loose under the metal band. The lovely cane chairs he bought from the south also suffered. My father had quite an eye for good furniture and he had saved up to buy a good piece of furniture every time he went on business in the south where good quality furniture was made. He used to travel often and he was a rising star of the railway bureau.

One morning, a rickshaw took my father to the emergency department of our local hospital after he had fainted at the riverbank café where he often went to have his soy milk. The café was really a small shop area in front of a bean-curd factory where my father would buy jellied bean curd and bring it back in a flask for our breakfast as a treat. The warm jellied bean curd, a sort of thick bean-curd soup, was delicious with a spot of chilli sauce and a splash of fragrant Chinese chives. That morning, our jellied bean-curd breakfast splashed all over the shop floor. What happened afterwards was a blur, and all I can remember was being taken with Meiling to go to see my father. He was half sitting in his bed, with drips and tubes and a big blue oxygen bottle somehow all attached to his bed. But that was too little and too late. This, I only learnt later when I was older. Had the doctors treated him earlier, he would not have died. But the doctors in our local hospital were either too involved in the political in-fighting which was endemic during the Cultural Revolution, or they were being sidelined and chose to stay at home on garden leave. Even the few doctors who actually worked at the time seemed to be so preoccupied with politics that it appeared that their treatment priorities were determined by what political factions their patients belonged to rather than by their medical conditions. The belated emergency treatment my father received only came when some senior figures in the railway bureau intervened.

My father looked pale, was a little breathless, but he managed to smile. 'Little potato skin,' he said to me fondly as he gently ran his hand over my face that was a little roughened by the chilly spring wind. He used to put moisturiser on for me: 'a little for the nose, a little for the cheeks,' he used to say. But he was too weak to do that. He told us to be good girls. Other people in the ward looked away or sighed. If I had been a little older, I would probably have guessed then just how ill my father was from the sudden privacy people gave us – locals then didn't have or respect privacy that much. That was our goodbye, and the next time I saw him was in the mortuary.

The mortuary was a one-storey row of rooms, with each room containing rows of beds covered in white. We were all outside waiting for the Liberation truck sent by the railway bureau to take my father and us to the crematorium. My sisters and I were each wearing a black band on our left arms. We all tried desperately to be grown-up, not to cry and not to be frightened. We shared a quiet sorrow and silent tears. 'Remember, you've promised to be brave for Mother.' Jing reminded me gently and wiped my tears away with her favourite sunflower handkerchief my father had bought her in Shanghai. I nodded, with some guilt for breaking my promise, and she smiled faintly, looking, at the age of 12, so grown-up and so dignified. To put on a brave face, Meiling and I started a game half-heartedly, only to be interrupted by the arrival of a group of mourners for other dead. Some of the mourners were wearing white from head to toe, a local custom, howling and yelling, as if they were competing with each other.

I had a last look at my father lying under a white sheet in the mortuary. He looked more radiant than he normally was, and under the white sheet, he was lying peacefully in his favourite blue *Zhongshan* suit, a Chinese tunic suit. As if to mark the era, my mother pinned on his jacket an enamelled badge of Chairman Mao's head, which was worn by most Chinese people at the time to mark their admiration and support for our 'Great leader'.

The wake was organised by my parents' friends and colleagues. Locals liked to have a meal after the funeral, to give the dead a send-off. The meal needed to be a feast, apparently so that the dead would have plenty to eat in another world. Having noodles was a must, as noodles would ensure a smooth journey to heaven and longevity in the next life. A big wok was being set up over the brick stove in Madam Guan's house. Using the bellows to get the fire going, Madam Guan was in her element. She brushed the big black iron wok with a damp brush, put in a generous amount of vegetable oil, and then threw in a handful of finely chopped spring onions when the oil was sizzling hot. After a few stirs, she filled the wok almost full with water and then put the wooden lid on; the lid was almost big enough to be a well cover. When the water was boiling, she put in a large quantity of noodles made by Madam Jiao. A good stir with her chopsticks and a couple of minutes later, she put in some cabbage leaves and some dried shrimps. She was making a noodle soup.

Madam Jiao's noodles were normally such a delicious treat, but I simply could not eat any that day. 'Eat some for your father's sake,' Madam Jiao said to Meiling and me. 'But we don't want him to have longevity in the next life, we want him here.' Meiling pushed away the bowls, in tears.

3

Cultural Re-education and the Lion's Head

My cousin Dong was a barefoot doctor. She was not a qualified doctor, and her training was limited to a few months in a medical school followed by a couple of months in a hospital. At least, that was how it was when she performed acupuncture on me.

I still have a clear picture of what her acupuncture kit was like. It looked impressive, with needles of all sizes: long, not so long, hair thin and not so thin. A diagram of a man with various acupoints marked was stuck neatly on the back of the lid. Her silver needles had helped cure many peasants and herdsmen in her village and nearby, she often told us with some considerable pride. She loved being a barefoot doctor, and visiting her patients in the paddy fields or the steppes gave her a real thrill.

Having disinfected a few needles with surgical spirit, she started to feel the acupoints in my hand. She then put two thin needles into acupoints in my left hand. Every five minutes or so, she would twist the needles a little before leaving them in their new positions for another five minutes or so. She was treating me for the terrible toothache I had when my new teeth tried to come through and some old ones refused to go. I remember that I was a little scared but didn't protest, as she had already bribed me with a small bag of Mongolian cheese she had brought back from her village. Interestingly enough, after the initial fright, I started to enjoy the sensation of the needles when cousin Dong twisted them. After thirty minutes or so, my toothache, miraculously, disappeared.

The Mongolian cheese was really bite-sized cubes of dried milk curd, which were very hard and tasted a little like a solid yoghurt. It was quite a popular snack for the Mongolians in our city, though most *Han*, who form the majority of Chinese, were not so fond of it. I liked the cubes because of my fondness for dairy products. Trying to chew them was lethal to the teeth, even without my tooth problems, so the best thing to do was to suck and taste. The proximity of our city to the steppes did mean that we had more milk products than most parts of China. The lovely peanut and milk toffee was mouth watering and deliciously chewy, and even most *Han* people liked it.

Dong arrived in her village at the age of seventeen, to receive re-education. Like all her friends from Beijing and other big cities, they were there to answer the call of Chairman Mao for school leavers 'to be re-educated by workers, peasants and soldiers'. Worried as their parents were, many young people had thought the whole thing would be fun and exciting, at least in the beginning. Dong's village was about twenty hours by train from Beijing, but only a few hours away from our city. During her holidays, Dong used to crowd our house with a group of her girl friends. There were so many of them that they camped out everywhere on our floor. My mother, gentle, good-natured and easygoing, was extremely popular with them, and our house was like an open house, with Dong's friends coming and going, often followed by friends of her brother Shengli. Shengli was a true child of the People's Republic of China, born in 1949, the year the republic was founded. His name Shengli, meaning 'victory', was one of the most popular names of his generation.

Our cousins and their friends from Beijing and further afield brought colour and life to our otherwise quiet Mongolian life, much welcomed after my father's death. They entertained us with tales from the big cities as well as the delicious food from their home towns. Eight Treasures was my favourite pickled vegetable assortment that was brought back from *Liubiju*,

Beijing's famous pickle and sauce shop, founded some four hundred years ago. Nothing but the finest-quality ingredients went into the pickle, with cubed lotus root, cucumber and carrots plus shredded lettuce, cabbage, runner beans and peppers, mixed with cooked peanuts and more. All were soaked in a unique blend of sauces including sugar, vinegar, salt and sesame oil. The end result was the most delicious pickle with an amazingly rich flavour and a smooth texture. Mixed with some steamed rice or sandwiched between two slices of steamed bread, it was a meal on its own.

Sharing our limited food supply, the young city people often took it upon themselves to do the cooking. Our small kitchen in the shed built by my father became a place for experiments. Nearly every meal was a surprise, with some meals being more pleasant than others. Jinmin's aubergine dish had to be one of the worst. He cut the aubergines into big chunks and then fried them with a little sesame oil and then simmered them in water. The end result was a soggy mush, which Jinmin received a lot of stick for. 'You've just wasted some really good aubergines,' Shengli shouted. 'You are supposed to be an artist,' Dong teased him as she set out to cook another aubergine dish. To be fair to Jinmin, aubergines always tasted better when fried with meat. But, with rationing, it was impossible to have meat very often, and besides, he only wanted to be a little creative. Dong's dish was inevitably much better. With two generous tablespoonfuls of sesame oil in a wok, Dong first deep-fried some thick aubergine slices which had been squeezed to reduce their water content. Then, she heated another wok containing one spoonful of oil, put in some chopped garlic when the oil was very hot and then added the partially cooked aubergine slices and a couple of tomatoes cut into quarters. A good stir, a little soy sauce and a pinch of salt, and the aubergines were ready a few minutes later. Dong was a really good cook and she knew it. 'Aubergine,' Jinmin shouted, standing on a chair with an old camera, as he was taking a picture of her proudly showing off her creation – 'aubergine' is the Chinese equivalent of saying 'cheese', which photographers ask people to say to make them smile for the camera.

Jinmin was an artistic young man and liked to play with his camera, which had belonged to his grandfather. Some of the pictures we have from when I was quite small were taken by him, and in quite a few of them I was wearing a badge depicting Chairman Mao. Jinmin was from a previously privileged background until his mother, who had once been a Russian interpreter to senior Chinese leaders, was sent to a labour camp together with his father who was a distinguished professor of art history. This was quite normal when I was growing up during the Cultural Revolution. Then, I was too young to know the significance of the event and at times even thought that it might be quite fun growing vegetables or feeding pigs on the farms to which many academics were sent. In fact, I was rather envious of my sister Yan when she went to some villages and army barracks with the school's Revolutionary Propaganda Troupe.

Yan had always wanted to have a musical instrument. My parents bought her an *erhu*, a two-stringed instrument played with a bow, when she was seven years old. She loved it and played it at lunchtimes, in the evenings and basically at any time she could. Most of the music scores we could buy at that time were of revolutionary songs or tunes from Peking operas with inevitably glorified heroines as the leading ladies. It was not difficult to see the strong influence of our first lady Madam Jiang Qing, Chairman Mao's wife and the self-anointed patron of the arts. 'You are doing really well,' Mr Wang, Madam Jiao's husband, told Yan at lunchtime one hot summer's day.

Yan seemed to be really pleased with the endorsement and played with even more enthusiasm, oblivious to the fact that Mr Wang was simply too polite to tell her that she was interrupting his siesta. She was perfecting a piece that she was due to perform in front of the whole school that afternoon. In our city, most people had long lunch breaks, particularly in the summer. Employers generally provided subsidised meals in the canteens, but the majority of people still preferred to cycle home for lunch, which would be followed by a siesta, except those who worked on shifts like my mother, who had started doing so after my father died. My other sisters and I had all developed the facility of turning down the volume of her music in our heads. You had to, especially when your sister even played music with chopsticks moving merrily over the edge of your glazed pickle jar. Poor Mr Wang, who had not yet developed that ability, had rather hoped that his praise would stop her practising. Obviously this was not so, and he was too nice to say any more.

It didn't take long before Yan grew out of her *erhu* and wanted to graduate to playing the accordion. Being an accordion player offered the ultimate high status in the school where membership of the propaganda troupe was already a status symbol. My father's death, on top of everything else, had made us a lot poorer. From being a two-salary household, we now had to manage on only my mother's salary. Accordions were expensive to buy and, with only my mother's salary, we could barely make ends meet, let alone afford one. Madam Zhang, a small, stocky lady with big bright eyes, came to the rescue one day, bringing us the school's accordion for Yan to practise on. Her arrival was heralded by her beautiful operatic voice.

Madam Zhang was kind but feisty, with a hot and fiery character just like the food from Sichuan, her hometown in the south-west of China. I remember that I was quite fascinated by the beautiful colour of a long string of hot red chilli peppers hanging outside her flat the first time I went to visit her. It was quite unusual to see these in our city as the locals were not particularly fond of spicy foods. The first time I had some really hot food was when my cousin Shengli was trying to impress us with *mapo doufu*, a hot spicy bean curd dish. Armed with a bottle of hot chilli sauce and a jar of fermented soya bean that one of his Sichuan friends had brought over, Shengli put a tablespoon of oil in the wok and then put in a sun-dried red chilli pepper broken into two. As the oil became hot, out came the fragrance of the chilli. He added some ground beef and stirred until it was cooked. He then added finely chopped ginger, garlic and spring onion, seasoned with two tablespoons of soy sauce, one spoonful of broad-bean sauce and one spoonful of fermented soya-bean sauce pre-mixed, together with a generous amount of chilli powder and other spices. Then he mixed in some small cubes of bean curd which had been quickly blanched in hot water and drained. A few minutes later, we had this hot, spicy, delicious and breathtaking dish. Served with boiled rice mixed with millet, it was out of this world. It is no wonder that *mapo doufu* is one of the most popular Chinese dishes.

It probably needs to be said that Shengli took a particular interest in cooking as he aspired to be the head of the cooking team in his village. That is what you did if you were ambitious, which a lot of those young people were. Dong loved her status as a barefoot doctor and one of her moments of glory was when she helped to deliver a baby when on an emergency call-out to a paddy field, in true barefoot doctor spirit. Our house was a little like an experimenting ground for Dong and Shengli, and Shengli liked to test his new dishes, which he called his repertoire, on us. One of the often-repeated dishes was caramelised potato chips. Considering that potatoes were one of the very few varieties of vegetables we had in our city, particularly in winter, it was a popular dish with us. When it was done well, a long lattice of caramelised sugar would be wrapped around each thick potato chip, giving it a crisp, sweet and tasty bite.

Yan took to the accordion like a duck to water (well, most ducks except ours). She progressed well and soon became the chief player of the propaganda troupe. Led by Madam Zhang, the troupe travelled to factories, army barracks, and across the Mongolian steppes to herdsmen and peasants in remote villages. She used to delight in telling us how she got all the young soldiers to sing to her music and how she moved herdsmen to tears with some old Mongolian tunes. Looking back, Yan's enjoyment of the spotlight and recognition went perhaps a little beyond the sheer excitement of a starry-eyed teenager.

With Yan's progress in music, my mother was encouraged, and she set out to find Yan a teacher, hoping that one day she would become a professional musician. Some work colleagues told my mother that the husband of another colleague was the first cellist of the Inner Mongolia Song and Dance Company, so my mother sought out this colleague, a beautiful and charming lady who asked her husband, Mr Zhou, who in turn talked to the chief accordion player in his orchestra. Mr Li, the chief accordion player, was a nice young man who agreed to be Yan's teacher. That's how it worked in Huhehot at that time, when everything seemed to be done through *guanxi*, this opaque network of personal relationships. Mr Li didn't charge for any tuition, which was quite the norm then. There was almost a code of barter of personal favours, unspoken but still clear to all the people concerned. I blamed myself for being cynical even to think like this, but that is how it appeared to my young eyes. Of course, I am not suggesting that Mr Li agreed to be Yan's teacher for any ulterior motive. He was genuinely kind and sympathetic, and he insisted on paying my mother for the eggs and geese she took to him occasionally. Being a *Hui*, he was particularly keen on the geese which my mother got by asking favours from yet another colleague who bought them from his parents' village nearby. That was part of the attraction of working at the railway bureau. I remember looking at those fresh eggs enviously as I helped my mother clean them and then wrap them up one by one in newspaper. Occasionally, I managed to persuade my mother to keep some for us, especially when we came across some double-yolk ones. We developed quite a skill at spotting double-yolk eggs, which were slightly elongated, with small, irregular protrusions in the middle. Of course we didn't always get it right.

At least my mother was able to repay Mr Li to some extent by acquiring the eggs for him. On the whole, my father's death had somehow taken away the potential of any personal favours my mother could return, and it took me a while to work out just why the gifts of baskets of apples disappeared, just like some of my father's friends. 'Why does nobody come to see us any more?' Yan, the extrovert of our family, used to protest sometimes, pouting unhappily. Her complaints were usually triggered by seeing people visiting Madam Jiao, our neighbour, with gifts of food. These occasional outbursts were always met by calm words from my mother, often followed by a quiet sigh.

There were, however, genuine and kind friends around – that is if my sister Jing and I didn't bar them from coming in. 'My mother's name is Zhang,' I told one man firmly. He had been outside our house twice already in one day, and what's more he was teasing me. I refused to be tricked into telling him what my mother's name really was, and in fact, I was quick to tell him that he was wrong, even though he was right. A thin man in his early forties, he looked harmless and quite fun, not in the least troubled or angered by my insistence on barring him from approaching our garden gate. He smiled and waited patiently, but could not resist teasing me, good-humouredly, from time to time. My young instinct told me that he was probably quite a nice man, but that was overridden by a sense of self-protection. Since my father's death, some adults in our neighbourhood had started to avoid my mother. 'Maybe they didn't know what to say,' my mother said, trying to make light of the situation, suggesting to me that not everybody knew how to deal with the newly bereaved. She was probably right, but somehow I felt that she was sad about this new isolation. In any case, she had so much to cope with and could hardly afford to dwell on such a thing. Her isolation, however, soon became apparent. It didn't take long before it spread to us that some old wives were telling tales that having anything to do with a young widow could bring misfortune. Soon, some boys and girls started to gang up against us. Stones started to fly at us and at our windows. Yan's status in the revolutionary propaganda troupe was no longer enough to protect her from being bullied. The more she protested, the more the gang would attack her and us. We were called names, and abuse was thrown at us, and no adults seemed to try to stop them, except for a few of our good neighbours. Most of the time, we had to rely on the Guans to chase away the gangs.

Now you can perhaps understand why I could not simply be welcoming to this nice man. 'She has grown into a little cute thing,' he said to my sister Jing, who murmured to me that he might be my parents' good friend Mr Deng. But she was not sure, because the Uncle Deng that she knew lived in Shanghai, a very long way away from us. I stared at him, part of me really wanted to like him, and part of me was resisting. I could not tell you what I was worried about, because I didn't know myself.

When she arrived, my mother's happiness at seeing Uncle Deng was written all over her face. They had not seen each other for a few years, not since Uncle Deng had been relocated back to Shanghai. He was on his way to a neighbouring city on a business trip, and he had stopped specially on the way to see my mother. As soon as she parked her Russian bicycle, a rather stylish lady's bike in green, she started to sort out supper straight away, while chatting enthusiastically to Uncle Deng. It was not long before my mother hauled a very embarrassed Jing and me out of hiding to greet Uncle Deng. Uncle Deng joked about our previous encounter as 'hide and seek', and offered us, once again, the delectable-looking crystallised fruit from Shanghai we had turned down earlier. A good cook, like many Shanghai men, he volunteered to cook us 'lion's head' for supper.

Lion's head is a famous dish from southern China and its origin can be traced back to the sixth century. With impressive meatballs shaped to resemble lion's heads, the dish has a smooth and delicious taste to it. Uncle Deng was soon chopping meat and vegetables effortlessly while chatting to my mother. Fine chopping is considered a prerequisite for a competent Chinese chef. With lion's head, the meat had to be chopped nearly as fine as minced meat, no easy task for any chef. Uncle Deng then mixed the finely chopped pork with equally finely chopped ginger, spring onion and garlic, then added soy sauce, corn-flour, pepper and rice wine. He beat an egg into the meat bowl and stirred thoroughly until the mixture was smooth before he set out to make good-sized meatballs. 'To be proper lion's heads, the meatballs need to be at least half a fist size,' he told Jing, who showed great interest in the cooking. He then deep-fried them in a wok until they were golden-brown and added some shallow-fried sliced carrots and Chinese cabbage to the wok with the meatballs, splashing in a generous amount of soy sauce, rice wine and some water. Leaving it to simmer on a medium heat, he prepared a cornflour mixture to thicken the sauce before finally sprinkling some finely chopped spring onions over the dish.

I have since had lion's head many times, in good restaurants and at banquets, but, somehow, Uncle Deng's have remained unbeatable and unforgettable, just like kind Uncle Deng himself. Reminiscing about them is in itself a delicious experience.

4

Milk Tea and the Red Guards

Two Friesian cows grazed happily on the meadows near the riverbank. Every morning, Mr Ma, our new neighbour, would go to the riverbank with a milk churn to milk the cows. Mr Ma, who always wore a round white skullcap, was very gentle with his cows, stroking them before and after he milked them. He often sang to the cows, and one day, I mustered up the courage to ask him why. He told me that his singing relaxed the cows, who would, in return, produce more and better milk. I must say that at that time I didn't understand much about the concept of relaxation, but I believed in Mr Ma, who came across as being pretty knowledgeable about his animals. Sometimes, I would follow him home, helping him to carry the small bamboo stool he used to sit on when milking. In return, Mr Ma would occasionally get a small ladle of the fresh milk, still slightly warm, from the churn, for me to drink. Even now, I can almost still taste this delicious, silky, raw milk smelling of the beautiful meadows on the riverbank. I used to drink it ever so slowly to make the whole experience last as long as possible.

Mr Ma used to take his churn of milk to a dairy the other side of the river on a wooden cart pulled by his small donkey. I knew that dairy well. In fact, my occasional presence at the dairy shop often attracted some curiosity and sympathy, and it was often assumed that I was a sick child. Milk, a luxury, was mostly reserved for the very young and for the seriously ill at that time. I often watched, through an open door, the cows being milked in the backyard. It was quite common in our city to have a shop at the front of the food-making premises and this dairy

39

was no exception. As soon as a churn was filled, the woman shop owner would bring it to the front of the shop, transfer some of the milk into an aluminium saucepan, and heat it over a coal stove. We were lucky to have fresh milk in our city, thanks to the proximity of the steppes, where the beautiful flora of the grasslands created such tasty milk and cheeses. As the milk heated, it sent out an aroma so tantalising that our mouths watered. As an occasional treat for me, my mother would buy a bowlful. She herself would go without; instead, she would happily watch me drinking from a small china bowl, carefully measured and filled with a ladle. The layer of cream floating on the surface was most delicious, and I would lose myself in my own world of milk drinking. Occasionally, I would remember to offer a sip to my mother, but was somehow quite relieved, often to my own shame later on, that she said no. 'Come on to the cart, little one,' a kind Mongolian lady once offered us a lift on her camel cart one day when we came out of the dairy, her eyes becoming narrower and her cheekbones more prominent with her smile. Her eyes were full of sympathy, for she thought I might be unwell. 'That's OK, then,' she said, when my mother told her that I was not ill. That day, I was a happy child, savouring the aftertaste of the delicious milk on a camel cart.

There were quite a few camel carts in our city, and the watermelon man used to come around on his cart every summer. I remember this thin man, with sun-tanned skin from working in the fields, sitting on his tall wooden cart laden with a pile of huge watermelons. He would stop near our poplar tree where his camel often enjoyed a snooze in the shade when he was busy selling the watermelons. He liked to smoke his pipe and, in between choosing the melons for his customers, he would sometimes replenish his pipe with some tobacco leaves which were skilfully rubbed into small bits to go in his pipe. To choose a good melon with the right texture, juiciness and ripeness is no easy task. Mr Wang, our amiable neighbour, was quite an expert. When choosing a melon, he would first look at the shape to examine its symmetry. Then he examined the complexion of the skin, looking for shine, smoothness and evenness by scrutinising the green skin and the black lines running through the skin. Satisfied, he then embarked on the third step, arguably the most difficult part. Holding a watermelon in his left hand, he used the palm of his right hand to tap strategically on the melon. 'Sound like your forehead, no, don't touch it,' he told me one day, pride in his expertise clear in his voice. 'It will be perfect if it sounds just like when you tap your chest.' He tapped his chest to enforce his point. I looked longingly at his melon, this perfectly shaped shiny oval thing in his hands. 'Have a piece.' He gave me a small triangular piece he skilfully cut with his special, very sharp, melon knife. It was absolutely divine.

The melon man would often cut several large melons into halves, and my mother would normally buy a half. On a hot summer's day, my mother would first put the half-melon into a container and fill the container with cold water, leaving the melon there for a while to cool it down. Then she would scoop the flesh of the melon out into four bowls, one for each of us girls, with her having the residual flesh next to the skin. With a little sugar sprinkled over it, the melon was truly delectable. 'Helmets for sale,' we would sometimes hear Guan Jie, better known as No. 8, shouting out next to the camel, wearing half a melon skin as a helmet. More often than not, he would be scolded by Madam Guan in her thick, throaty Manchurian accent between her cigarette puffs.

My first Mongolian tea was an elaborate affair. Having at last plucked up the courage to approach the Mas, who largely liked to keep themselves to themselves and socialise mostly with other *Huis* from the nearby Muslim district, my mother was delighted when they agreed to sell her some milk from time to time. That was all we could afford anyway. With a small piece of brick tea she had just bought, my mother, pleased with our fresh milk, prepared to make the Mongolian tea. First, she got out a silver teapot from behind a shoe box, unwrapping the many pieces of newspaper surrounding it. She then dusted the teapot with a damp piece of soft cloth. Having rinsed it thoroughly, she then put it on top of our round dining table. It was almost like a ritual.

The fact was that she had not seen this silver teapot for a long time, not in daylight anyway. It was one of the very few family heirlooms she had, and it had belonged to her great-great-grandmother who had been the daughter of a Mongolian nobleman. She rarely talked about the past and, thinking about it now, I can still see, in her bright eyes, a sense of nostalgia, happiness mixed with a certain sadness, when she was making the milk tea.

She first brought the milk to the boil, then she boiled about double the quantity of water. Putting the brick tea, a sort of fermented black tea pressed into the shape of a brick, into boiling water, she added a little salt before pouring it all into the milk pan. She then brought the mixture to the boil before she poured it slowly and carefully into the silver teapot. Tea was now ready to be served. One by one, she gave us each a bowl of Mongolian tea, just like Mongolians would do in their yurts. Accompanied by toasted millet, the tea, with its subtle fragrance, was truly delightful. 'Rather go without food for a day than without tea' was an old Mongolian saying, and I now understood why.

I always liked tea and started to drink it when I was quite young. Too young really, Madam Song, one of mother's colleagues said. In her view, that was why I was not growing bigger and taller. 'Tea is good for the digestion, but I reckon it has taken all the nutrients away from her,' she told my mother authoritatively. In spite of that, she still kept on offering me tea every time I went to see my mother at work. 'Hello, little No. 4,' she would call me in the same way as Madam Guan, peering over her glasses. I didn't roll my eyes at her, like I did with Madam Guan. In fact, it was often the opposite. 'Auntie Song,' I called her sweetly. It has to be said that my behaviour was not influenced by her being a powerful lady married to the railway bureau's chief army representative, but it certainly had a lot to do with my fondness of tea.

In our city, being an army representative was to be of high status indeed, and all the key divisions and companies under the railway bureau had army representatives. We had them, I heard Madam Song once explaining to my sister Jing, because of the strategic importance of our city and of our railway network. I faintly understood the bit she mentioned about our railway network's link to Outer Mongolia, the name used in our city for the People's Republic of Mongolia, as I had seen some important-looking Mongolian men coming through the station's VIP lounge to music played by the army band.

Auntie Song was not my real aunt, but, in our city, it was considered polite to call your parents' colleagues, friends or close neighbours of their generation aunts and uncles. Almost immediately after she saw me, she would get out from her desk drawer a small tin of jasmine tea. Taking a pinch of tea leaves with her rather plump fingers and putting them in what normally was a glass jar of some sort, she would then pour some boiled water from the office's thermos flask over them. I used to watch closely as she poured the water into the jar and was fascinated by how the tea leaves swam around until they settled to the bottom of

43

the jar, with only perhaps a few jasmine leaves floating on top. Before I took my first sip, I would often inhale the beautiful fragrance of the tea. Sometimes, if I was lucky, Auntie Song would offer me a bite of her tea egg. Tea eggs are soft-boiled eggs, peeled and then boiled again in a mixture of water, soy sauce, tea leaves, star anise, Chinese pepper and a little salt. They would be left in the sauce overnight, and tasted delicious the next day.

We did not grow tea in Huhehot, so all our tea came from the south. Apart from brick tea, the other most common tea we had was jasmine tea. Jasmine tea is a popular tea with people in the north and its popularity started some two hundred years ago. Very occasionally, my mother would buy *Longjing* tea, a well-known green tea from near the West Lake in Zhejiang province. 'I want to work in a tea shop when I grow up,' I told my mother every time I went to a tea shop with her. I can still remember this tea shop in a narrow alley, with tea leaves stored in air-tight jars, all neatly displayed on an old elm table. A tiny lady skilfully wrapped up the tea leaves in a piece of pink and a piece of white paper after weighing them carefully on an old-fashioned scale. The rustic smell of the wood and the fragrance of the teas was delightful. When making green tea, my mother often added a few *gouqi* berries in it. *Gouqi* berries are bright red dried berries from Ningxia in northern China, and are one of the world's most powerful and highly concentrated antioxidants.

Like milk tea, sweets were also very much a treat. 'One, two, three, that's it,' Meiling said, almost breathlessly, after giving me yet another piggyback ride. We were on the way back from visiting an art exhibition in the city museum, an impressive two-storey white building with a sculpture of a galloping horse on top. I had been there many times now with Meiling since she took up painting. The museum was a couple of miles away from our home, but sometimes it felt like a long march, especially on the way home when we were tired and hungry. There was a bus service, but it was not very frequent. In any case, Meiling and I chose to save our money to buy sweets from the shop near the museum. 'So we had a windfall again today?' a large-framed lady in her forties used to tease us every time we went into her shop. In spite of her teasing, she was a patient lady and often looked on, with some bemusement, as Meiling and I studied her sweets with the intensity and concentration of art connoisseurs examining some potentially priceless art works. Some of her sweets were in wooden display boxes on the counter and some, often the more expensive ones, were displayed tantalisingly in large glass jars on the shelves behind the counter. I always had a preference for more expensive milk-based sweets, with the mouthwatering milk-and-peanut toffee being my favourite, while Meiling was often tempted by fruit-flavoured sweets. Not that she didn't like the delicious milk sweets, but to a large extent she was lured by the pretty colours of the fruit sweets and their colourful wrappings. Since she had started collecting the wrappings lately, our decisions, already much restricted by our small budget, were made even harder, but we both had learnt long ago how to make compromises. After all, any sweets, never mind whether they were milk sweets or fruit sweets, were a great treat for us, and the act of choosing was a delicious experience in itself.

Our sweets experience was often made even sweeter by having a lift on the way home. Sometimes, we would be given a lift on a cart, and it could be a horse cart, an ox cart, a donkey cart, a mule cart or a camel cart. There were many carts in our city, and because of this, some new posts were being set up by the city government to control the animal droppings in the street, which were quite a serious environmental problem. Meiling and I laughed our heads off when Guan No. 5 proudly told us how she had stopped a farmer for failing to give his horse a bag to wear around its bottom. No. 5, with the enthusiasm of a new recruit, was not at all pleased with us not taking her job seriously. To her, we were almost committing a sort of blasphemy towards her hard-to-get job.

It didn't take long for me to develop a sixth sense to identify the cart driver who was most likely to say yes to us. Most of the time, we were lucky and were given a lift without any fuss. Most cart drivers, in fact, seemed to enjoy having us on their carts, and they found it entertaining to listen to Meiling and me reading all the revolutionary slogans. There were plenty of those slogans in our city, on the red flags flying in the street and on the concrete notice boards around every neighbourhood. 'You, little potatoes, know so much?' Some cart drivers found it incredible that we already knew so many complicated and difficult words. 'Carry the proletarian Cultural Revolution to the end!' I read out loud, encouraged by the praise of the cart drivers and to the amusement of some cyclists who would turn their heads while riding, and could not resist the temptation to tease us. The truth was that I had little idea of what I was reading, and I very much doubt, looking back now, whether all the adults fully understood all the slogans, which changed more frequently than one could keep up with. Reading slogans nevertheless formed part of my early education, and it was fair to say that the literacy level Meiling and I reached was far more advanced than others in our age group. My mother had little spare time, between working full time and trying to run our home. But whenever she could, she would take Meiling and me out, even just going to buy food together. Whenever she could, she would teach us to read new characters on the flags and bulletins around every street corner. Normally I would sit on the front bar of my father's old bicycle while Meiling sat on the back seat. Because of her height, getting on to the back seat was somewhat hit-and-miss for Meiling when the bicycle was in motion. Often she would be left holding precariously on to the back seat with her hands and chest with her legs dangling behind.

It was a summer's day when Meiling painted her first water-colour. Seated at a small square table in the shade of our poplar tree, she copied a painting of a girl holding an umbrella. It was a difficult painting for a beginner, but Meiling really enjoyed it. Having a couple of new brushes and a brand-new box of water-colours of her very own, it seemed, was pleasure enough for her. My mother is very artistic, and whenever she came across a woman artist, musician or writer, her admiration was apparent. 'That's our spiritual food,' she used to say about art, music and literature. But having spiritual food was not all that was on her mind. We had to be outstanding at something, she often said to us, otherwise we could not even get a job like the one Guan No. 5 had got. After all, Mr Guan had had to pull some strings even to get his daughter the job monitoring animal droppings.

We had recently had some new additions to our house. Some chicks had just hatched out of their shells. Timidly and care-fully, we helped them to settle in their bed, a big circular woven bamboo board. Jing and Meiling were good at helping the chicks and their mother to adjust to their new life. I helped by putting a sheet of cotton around the edge of the bamboo board and putting water in a couple of small bottle caps. Most of our neigh bours raised chickens at that time, as it was such an invaluable addition to our rationing. In our row of seven terraced houses, there were about five families, I recall, that had chickens at one time or another. Before the arrival of the chicks, we had two hens and a cockerel that had the most beautiful feathers and a resonant crowing. During the daytime, our chickens roamed leisurely in our front garden, or our courtyard, as we often called it. Sometimes, they would wander daringly into the courtyards of our neighbours, only to be shooed back, subtly or sometimes not so subtly, to where they belonged. There were some unwritten rules, it seemed, in our row of terraces that every family should try its hardest to keep its fowl in its own garden. Thinking about it now, it is quite incredible that, considering the limited space we all had, most of the neighbours in our row managed to get on quite well, with little shouting across the fences. Sometimes, our chickens, in adventurous mood, would march across the road and up to the wood near the river, a sociable place for chickens to mix in their own groups and hopefully find some worms to eat to supplement the limited millet supply they shared with us. Often, when evening fell and when they were too carried away with socialising, we would have to go and chase them back to their house, the now rather derelict duck house my father had built a few years ago, before the foxes found them.

The arrival of our yellow fluffy chicks brought great delight to us, and in particular to Meiling, as the mother hen was one she had brought back to life by nursing her when she caught severe avian flu, which happened occasionally in our neighbourhood at that time. The flu had made the hen lose her appetite and damaged her neck and head. It had been quite scary to see her walking around literally like a headless chicken, with head and neck perpetually turning backwards and upwards. Pecked at by the other two chickens, she was often covered in black and blue bruises. Meiling took on the job of nursing her. Having found an old cardboard box, she provided the hen with her own space. She would then feed the hen separately with millet and water. Struggling to see, because of her head and neck, the hen would be spoon fed by Meiling who religiously mixed into the food a small dose of antibiotics she had ground to a powder. The antibiotics were bought at our local pharmacy, which sold not only Chinese herbal medicine but also a small selection of western medicines. Meiling's efforts were not in vain, and after a period of intense nursing and TLC, the hen made a full recovery with her head and neck back in the right positions and her comb a healthy red. What is more, as if to reward Meiling, the first time egg she laid after her recovery was double-yoked. To make the egg last as long as possible, Meiling pickled it. Washing a glass jar thoroughly, she put the egg in and then added a generous amount of salt before filling the jar with cold water. She then screwed the lid on as tightly as she could, and then placed the jar in a prominent position on the top shelf of our bookcase.

Jing had taken on the role of a parent since my father's death. 'We're each going to have a drawer and a shelf,' she announced one day when my mother was on a weekend shift, with a quiet authority which, thinking about it now, was pretty impressive for a teenager. She was very tidy, just like my father, and to live in a small terraced house like ours, that tidiness was an invaluable bonus and in fact, a necessity. Having just cleaned and tidied up the walnut desk and the bookcase, she set some rules. 'The long desk drawer in the middle will be Mother's and you can choose any other one you like, provided you put as much of your stuff in there as possible,' she told us with some considerable clarity. So far and so good. Her new regime was greeted with enthusiasm by Meiling and me, who were both quite excited about having our own space. In fact, Meiling had already set her sights on the top shelf where the pickled-egg jar proudly sat. But Yan, who had so far remained uncharacteristically quiet, also wanted to have the top shelf. In fact, she made it quite clear that she was not going to buy in to the new regime if she could not have the top shelf. 'You should let Meiling choose first, because she is younger,' Jing tried to talk Yan out of it. 'But in that case, you should let me have what I want, because you're older,' Yan retorted, testing Jing's management skills to the limit. As it happened, I had set my eye on a large round bamboo basket, which Jing had gladly endorsed. So, she offered my shelf to Yan, who was more than pleased to have two shelves, even though the top shelf went to a very happy Meiling.

The happy atmosphere was soon broken by a squawking from our cockerel. Far from its usual resonant crowing, this was an unbearably painful growl. Something was not right, and we all instinctively rushed to our front door. In front of us was Niu, an aggressive and beefy 14-year-old boy from the neighbourhood, holding our cockerel tightly under his left armpit and pressing it so tight that the poor creature was on the point of choking. Unceremoniously and almost violently, he plucked the feathers from the cockerel's tail. 'You stop there,' he barked at Yan, who had just picked up a broom and was about to lash out at him. Jing stopped Yan, while comforting Meiling who was in tears, distraught to see the cockerel suffering. I don't know where I found the strength from but I gave the loudest cry I could. My yell surprised and shocked Niu temporarily and in his moment of brief distraction, the cockerel flew out from under his arm. Having recovered from its ordeal remarkably quickly and as if to show gratitude to and solidarity with us, the cockerel gave one of its most resonant crows before flying bravely and purpose-fully into the direction of Niu's face. For solidarity and perhaps for fun, both our hens joined in to attack Niu, as he bent down to pick up the feathers falling on the ground. 'He's covered in shit,' Guan No. 8, who could rarely resist involving himself in such a scene, cheered, as Niu, literally henpecked, struggled to recover the feathers and more importantly, his loss of face.

Our cockerel was not the only thing to be picked on. 'Come on,' flat-faced Hao Ping shouted at me. 'Come and join the triangle fight,' she challenged me. The triangle fight was a children's game, with each player hopping while trying to knock down their opponents. The trick was to avoid being knocked over, and therefore out of the game, and whoever survived the longest would win. It was during a break at school when Flat Face challenged me. I enjoyed school and loved literacy and arithmetic, a welcome change after the boredom at the kindergarten Meiling and I always used to run away from. In our city, children started school between the ages of seven and eight, and before that, most of us would have gone to the kindergarten, a combination of play school and pre-school. I still remember sitting in this playroom-cum-classroom and watching Teacher Guo, a kindergarten teacher, writing out the Chinese character 'fire'. 'Doesn't it look like a flame?' she asked, writing out, painstakingly and deliberately slowly, every stroke of the character. She looked quite pleased with herself for explaining so well one of the Chinese characters evolved from pictographs, but her displeasure was apparent when she spotted that I was not nodding as enthusiastically as some of my peers. Not that I was not interested in the subject – on the contrary, I was fascinated when my mother first told Meiling and me the story of how the ancient Chinese recorded events on knotted cords and then on tortoise shells some three thousand years ago. I was simply bored, but it was not the done thing to say to your teacher that all the characters she was teaching were too basic. I knew even as a six-year-old that would amount to disrespect and arrogance, the two worst possible offences. Watching her writing on the blackboard was deeply boring, only the screeching of the chalk kept my mind from wandering too far. I could not wait to leave the kindergarten.

School was a more interesting proposition, but it was far from ideal. Glass was often broken by vandals, and many windows had to be boarded up to stop the extreme cold from the howling, freezing wind. With the electricity supply often interrupted, the classrooms could be dark and miserable. To cope with the lack of teachers and the condition of the class-rooms, a rota system was introduced, with Meiling's year having classes for half a day and my year having classes for the other half of the day. This enabled the school to just about keep a few rooms weather-proof and moderately light.

Flat Face was a ringleader in my year. Boisterous and aggres-sive, she would pick on both girls and boys. Her usual tactic was to spit at, and pull the hair of, whoever she fancied picking on, until the victim became her loyal follower. I was soon iden-tified as her prey, partly because I didn't join in her spitting and partly because she didn't like the fact that the teachers praised me for my good literacy and maths. As if being spat on by her and her gang of followers was not enough punishment, she started to isolate me. Whoever dared to talk to me risked being ostracised. I put on a brave face every time she excluded me from any game, and sometimes even pretended that I didn't notice, but deep down, I longed to join in.

Flat Face's invitation to join the triangle fight therefore rather surprised me, and I was even a little suspicious. My eagerness to be part of the gang, however, overtook my caution and I joined in. At first, all was well. Flat Face even set out to protect me from an attack from some opponents. Then something happened, and I found myself in agony lying next to a kerb, unable to move or bend my left arm. 'Stop pretending,' one of Flat Face's loyal followers shouted, to the cheers of some other followers, some of whom started spitting. I was in too much pain to move. 'You idiots,' came a shout, and Lanlan, another classmate, came to my rescue.

Lanlan, with rosy complexion and brown eyes, was Mr Ma's daughter. Being something of an outsider herself, she rarely joined in any games started by Flat Face. So far, Flat Face hadn't dared to start on Lanlan, as she was fearful of her three big brothers. It was after school and Lanlan convinced me that I should come home with her and her brothers for Mr Ma to help put my arm right. He was once a shepherd, she said, and learnt his skill through setting the bones and tendons of lambs when they injured themselves by slipping on the hills.

Mrs Ma smiled at me sympathetically as Lanlan told her of my ordeal. We were in their small front-room-cum-kitchen and she was making a lamb soup. She put lamb cut into cubes into a saucepan of boiling water. After a few minutes, she drained the meat, so that the meat was rid of debris and its raw smell. She then heated some vegetable oil in a wok, threw in a few large pre-cut pieces of ginger into the heated oil, and added the lamb cubes. Filling the wok with eight big bowls of water, she poured some rice wine into the wok before finally adding some *gouqi* berries. 'An hour of simmering, and it will be done,' Mrs Ma told me, registering my interest in her cooking.

As the delicious smell of the simmering soup wafted through the room Mr Ma worked at my arm, twisting and pulling until he had manoeuvred the dislocated joint bone back into its socket. The pain was so immense that tears just streamed down my cheeks. Feeling sorry for me, Mrs Ma gave me a bowl of freshly cooked lamb soup. 'Go on, have some. It will be good for you,' she said to me. I was embarrassed, and anxious not to come across as being greedy. But the lamb soup smelt good, looked good and tasted good as well.

'Having milk and making Mongolian tea in a fancy teapot?' a Red Guard marched in through our front door unannounced. His fellow Red Guard was looking, disapprovingly, at Meiling's watercolour, which we had put on the wall. 'Too bourgeois,' the first Red Guard, a youth of 16 or so, said, getting Mao's little red book out of a pocket of his old green army uniform. He was not in the army, and like many activists, or young revolutionaries as they were called at that time, he wore the uniform to make himself look more important than he was. After all, Auntie Song's husband, the chief army representative, was always in his army uniform.

Apparently, the two Red Guards had been tipped off by Guan No. 4 about our Mongolian tea, which I had mentioned to No. 8, probably to show off. He in turn had told his brother who decided to ingratiate himself with those revolutionary activists. It was too bourgeois and indulgent to do such a thing, and we should be, at least, reprimanded, the two young men told us in no uncertain terms. My mother should do self-criticism for bringing up her children in such a decadent way. My mother nodded and listened attentively when they told her off, which was the best thing to do at that time. In fact, that was the only thing to do if my mother didn't want to get into further trouble. To confront them or argue might bring disastrous consequences. 'Long live Chairman Mao,' the two men said loudly as they walked to our door. They stopped abruptly when the second man spotted a pair of my mother's high-heeled shoes. My mother had not dared to wear this beautiful pair of leather shoes for a long time, in fact I could not remember ever having seen her wearing them. Meiling and I had spotted them when my mother had got the teapot out. We could not resist putting them on, although they were far too big for either of us, and our imaginations took us to great mansions and theatres, in exquisite Chinese robes and beautiful high-heeled shoes. Our world of fantasy was brought to an abrupt end when the second Red Guard grabbed the axe my mother used to cut kindling wood for our stove. He cut off the heels and, as if that was not enough, he threw the heels into the stove.

That day, my mother was not in the mood to cook, and all we had was a bit of pickle, some steamed sweetcorn buns and a millet porridge.

5

Spring Festival and Four Happiness

Jing was bribing Meiling and me with *matang*, a sesame-coated sweet. 'I'll give you a few more after you clean this window,' she said, tempting us with a few more pieces of the sticky sweet. We were giving the house a spring clean in preparation for the 'Small New Year', a prelude to the main Chinese New Year or Spring Festival.

The Small New Year, normally about a week before the New Year proper, is an important date on the lunar calendar. Apart from spring cleaning, it is traditional to make an offering to the Heavenly God of Cooking. 'Save some sweets for him,' Madam Guan shouted across the fence, between the jobs of supervising her children and cooking. 'Otherwise, he will rubbish us in heaven, and then we might have nothing to eat next year,' she declared, quite adamant. Madam Guan was pretty superstitious and she told Meiling and me off when we made faces at a bowl of noodle soup that she had cooked religiously to offer to the heavenly god. It was not just any old noodle soup, she said to Jing, who appeared more receptive, it was a special noodle soup with noodles made of a mixture of white flour, bean flour and ground sweet potato flour.

My mother cooked vegetable meatballs for us for the Small New Year. She mixed grated potato and carrot, finely chopped Chinese chives and spring onions together in a large bowl, added an egg and then seasoned the mixture with salt and pepper. She then put some white flour into a separate bowl, added some cold water and mixed it thoroughly with a pair of bamboo chopsticks until the batter was smooth and had the consistency of thin cream. She then poured this batter into the vegetable bowl and stirred it. Taking a tablespoonful of the mixture each time, using her favourite spoon, she rolled the mixture into meatballs. Heating a generous amount of vegetable oil in the wok, she put the meatballs into the wok once the oil had become very hot. She turned them over from time to time to avoid over-browning, and the resulting sizzling hot meatballs were golden and delicious.

Our enjoyment of the meatballs was interrupted by a loud cry from Meiling. She was standing by an elm dresser my father had bought from Shanghai, and my parents' favourite blue enamel mug was rolling on to the floor. My mother had filled the mug with boiling water so that by the time we finished our meatballs, we could have some boiled water at the right temperature to drink, and she had deliberately put the mug out of the reach of Meiling and me, so she had thought, to avoid accidents.

Drinking hot water was the norm at that time and it was meant to be good for your *yin* and *yang*. Another reason that we drank hot water all the time was that cold water directly from the tap or well was not clean enough to drink. Having a tap and running water in our house was quite a recent thing. For some time now, a number of resourceful neighbours had been connecting pipes from our communal water tap to their own houses. The Guans were among the first to do this. I still remember the first time I saw Madam Guan proudly filling her copper kettle directly with the water running out of this magical red tap inside her house. She even indulged me and allowed me to fill our cast-iron kettle with water from her tap, which was quite an exhilarating experience. My mother didn't say much, I recall, when I told her about my experience with Madam Guan's lovely red tap as she filled our large, rounded glazed urn, except that she told me I should not trouble the Guans too much with their tap. I nodded, though I thought it would help my mother a great deal if we occasionally 'troubled' the Guans. With the communal tap some two hundred metres away from our house, Mother often struggled when she fetched water, particularly when the ground was icy near the tap, which happened often in winter. An image that features rather prominently in my memory is Mother struggling to balance, on her slight shoulders, a bamboo yoke with a large aluminium bucket filled with water hung on each end. One day, I remember, she was exceptionally quiet and sad when she came back with her buckets half empty. I later learnt that Niu, the aggressive cockerel-feather poacher, had deliberately run into her and made her lose her balance. At least that had now all become something of the past and, with our new tap, my mother no longer needed to go through all this. Our tap, though not as good as the Guans' red one, was a delight and had been put in by kind Mr Guo, the husband of the Guans' eldest daughter, No. 1. After the incident with Niu, Madam Guan promised to help my mother, but it was quite some time before Mr Guo, a plumber working for a water company, managed to gather enough scrap for our fitting. That was what people in our city did then, as you could barely get anything from any hardware shop.

Meiling's cry made my mother immediately drop everything. Meiling had been badly scalded. With amazing speed, my mother poured a generous amount of cooking oil into her left hand and then quickly smeared it all over Meiling's face and neck. Time was of the essence, and she had learnt this method of dealing with burns from our friend Zhuji's grandfather. 'The girl won't have any scars when she grows up,' Zhuji's grandfather consoled my mother several days later when he saw Meiling's face covered in black burnt skin. 'I'll frighten anybody who dares to bully my sister,' Meiling told the Guans. Even naughty No. 8 became a little wary of Meiling, who walked around with her mask of burnt skin, dark, frightening and almost ghost-like. I am still not sure whether it was Meiling's mask or whether it was just a coincidence, but the bullying eased off a little at that time, and Flat Face and her followers seemed to focus on somebody else. Meiling's mask disappeared after a month or so, and thanks to my mother's quick wit, her face had recovered without a scar.

I was in my element when we started doing arithmetic and learning the abacus in school. I had this fascination with the abacus, and loved the clicking sound of the moving beads. The lady in the Chinese herbal medicine shop across the river always looked very ladylike whenever she moved the delicate white beads on her dainty white abacus, adding up the cost of each herb ingredient included in every prescription. Auntie Song was more aggressive with hers, moving the big beads on her chunky black abacus very quickly, like any efficient accountant would do. Occasionally, while having the tea she offered me in her office, I was allowed to use her abacus. Sometimes, when she was in a really good mood, she would test me with addition and subtraction problems on her abacus.

'You little abacus,' came the shrieking voice of Flat Face back at school. Unable to cope with doing calculations on abacus during revision time, Flat Face was infuriated by the way I moved the beads up and down quickly. I ignored her abuse, 'little abacus' being a derogatory name in our city, and carried on with my homework. My reaction, or, rather, lack of it, outraged her, and she picked up my abacus and smashed it on the floor. Seeing the beads of my father's broken abacus running all over the floor was too much for me to bear. I grabbed Flat Face and smacked her in the face. There was an absolute silence in the classroom, and everybody was totally taken by surprise, not least myself. Everybody, including Flat Face's loyal followers, watched in awe as I calmly picked up the beads of my abacus, with Flat Face standing in a corner in shock and reeling from the utter loss of face. To her, the loss of face was ultimately worse than the pain from the smacking, and her resentment was written all over her. That incident performed miracles. As if a great dark cloud had been lifted, from that day onward, school became a more enjoyable place for me.

Cousin Shengli did not become the head of the cooking team as he had hoped, but he became the proud driver of the 'Iron Ox' of his village, the one and the only driver, he told us during his winter holiday. Everybody seemed to be really excited, but I didn't really understand what an iron ox, a name used in our city for a tractor, was all about. Shengli talked enthusiastically with his friends about modernisation and efficiency, but I could not fully understand it at all. 'He only gives lifts to the prettiest girls in our village,' his friend Lin teased him in front of a curious me. 'Not t-t-t-true,' Shengli stammered a little. He didn't normally stammer, and, as I remember, his stammer only occurred when he was either extremely embarrassed or very excited. Perhaps to stop his friend teasing him further or to distract me from taking in such grown-up talk, Shengli turned his attention to me. 'The iron ox ploughs a lot faster and better than any old yellow ox in our village,' he explained, having recovered from his stammering. 'So does that mean you will have more food to bring back from your village, then?' My simplistic question made everybody laugh.

The head of the cooking team in their village was Lin. 'Only because of your chilli,' Shengli teased him, not admitting defeat easily. Lin indeed used a lot of chilli in his cooking. My first memory of him was seeing him arriving at our house with a string of dried red chilli peppers attached to his luggage, with his small beady eyes smiling behind his big glasses. In fact, a string of red chillies was a colourful and must-have accessory to his luggage every time he came back from his home in Hunan. His food was often hot and spicy, sometimes almost too pungent to bear. It was amazing how fast our palates adjusted, though. The first mouthful, which often required a little bravery to take, soon led you to want to have more and more. Lin's food was a little addictive, the more you ate, the more you wanted to eat.

Lin was from Chairman Mao's home town in Hunan province, something that he was very proud of. He talked fast, particularly when excited, with some words often lost in his thick Hunan accent, which was entertaining and sometimes incomprehensible. In a country as vast as China, regional accents and dialects vary a lot. Sometimes, the variations go beyond the conventional boundaries. Meiling and I used to find it amusing to listen to our cousins' friends arguing. When all was calm, everybody spoke *Putonghua*, standard Chinese, albeit with a little accent, and there was nothing unusual about that. At the time of argument, it was quite a different scene. It was less fun to see the Beijing gang, who prided themselves on speaking the Chinese equivalent of the 'Queen's English', arguing among themselves, because they simply continued the argument in *Putonghua*. The Shanghai gang were more entertaining, arguing in their Shanghai dialect, which we barely understood, at a supersonic speed, while the hot-tempered Sichuan and Hunan gang were most expressive with their dialect, highly atmospheric, with plenty of drama in the tones. The best entertainment, though, was when the Shanghai gang and the Sichuan and Hunan gang argued with each other in their separate dialects. Not fully understanding each other didn't seem to matter, and it was a question of who could shout the loudest. The arguments could sometimes go a little too far with sensitive subjects. One of the most heated arguments I remember was when two members of the Beijing gang retaliated by shouting abuse at the southerners for being too bloody smart for their own good after one of the Hunan gang said that northerners were coarse and lazy. That argument only stopped when Madam Guan shouted over the fence, saying that they all deserved to be chucked out, and she was going to tell my mother to do so as soon as she came back from work.

I loved watching Lin cooking. It was exciting to watch him sharpening the knife skilfully on the edge of our stone water urn, as part of his cooking ritual. To my young eyes, Lin was the ultimate master chef. When he was in charge of the kitchen, everybody involved in helping understood that only the highest standard was acceptable. Lin's signature dish was the Dongan chicken, a famous dish from his home town and one whose origin could be traced back a thousand years. Rinsing the whole chicken thoroughly before putting it into a big saucepan to boil for 8 to 10 minutes, he would then drain it and chop off the head, neck and feet for other uses. He then separated the breasts and legs and de-boned the chicken, and then cut the main part of the chicken into strips about two inches long and half an inch wide. Like Uncle Deng with his lion's head, Lin was brilliant at preparing food. With most Chinese cooking, preparation is the most demanding and time-consuming part.

With his sharpened knife, he cut the chicken in the direction which took most advantage of the texture. He then finely chopped ginger, spring onion and a few red chillies. Putting a generous lump of lard into a preheated wok, Lin waited till it was melted and bubbling. He then threw in the chicken strips, ginger and chillies, and started stirring. Adding some vinegar and Shaoxing rice wine, he seasoned it with salt and pepper and then added some clear chicken stock. After bringing it to the boil, he simmered it for a few minutes before finally adding some pre-mixed cornflour paste to the wok. Giving it a good stir, he then brought the chicken and sauce to the boil once more before splashing in a few drops of sesame oil.

Watching Lin cook was like watching an artist creating a work of art, and between cooking different dishes he often paused, as if to compose himself. My occasional moaning that I was hungry, often made worse by the delicious cooking smells, did nothing to distract him from creating his masterpieces, and he carried on as if he were in a different world. But the Dongan chicken was always worth waiting for, succulent, packed with flavour and simply addictive. The problem was that there was never enough there to let us really tuck in.

Lin's repertoire was not limited to Hunan dishes; he was also rather fond of cooking spicy Sichuan dishes. With a prized piece of beef that cousin Dong had brought back from the steppes, part of a barter payment to her for her work as a barefoot doctor, Lin was only too happy. Even with our proximity to the steppes, beef was a luxury and only very occasionally could we buy braised beef from a food store across the river. To be a *sous-chef* to him was no easy task, since any slight transgression would be noted. Even Shengli was once severely reprimanded for not chopping the spring onions well enough. It was not a simple beef stew that Lin was to cook, rather it was boiled beef in the

Sichuan style. Lin liked to cook something different on each occasion.

Taking the sliced beef, Lin mixed it with salt, soy sauce and cornflour to make it tasty and tender. He then fried a chilli until it was golden brown, adding chilli sauce, thick broad bean sauce and a few whole Chinese peppercorns. He then added spring onion, asparagus and lettuce that had been washed and chopped, poured in beef stock and waited for it to boil, and then added the beef slices and simmered the mixture until the meat was cooked. Finally he added more chilli oil before it was time to serve. The beef, tender and fresh, had the most pungent and aromatic taste.

It must sound as though we were having feasts every day, and, in a way, I suppose we were. We all loved food, no matter which part of China we were from, and we were all keen to try and make something special out of our limited supplies. Every meal was an occasion, with the kitchen sounding like an orchestra with chopping and frying variations. We all, old and young, sat down together for our meals, to share the delicious if quite small amount of food. Our cousins and their circle of friends, who had all come to our area to answer the call of Chairman Mao, were now like an extended family to us; they all took it upon themselves to help, and some truly delicious meals were born out of their rivalry, all perfectly friendly of course. Through their cooking, they each brought a piece of their home town to us.

Red lanterns blew merrily in the chilly wind, amid the banging of firecrackers. The lanterns, cheerful and bright, lit up a little the otherwise dim and grey-looking houses in our neighbourhood. My mother was at my father's walnut desk, busy making

Chinese scrolls while Meiling was helping her by cutting strips out of a large sheet of red paper. Red is a colour traditionally used for weddings, festivals and celebrations, and a lucky colour for Chinese people. Meiling took her task very seriously, and neatly produced many strips, about as wide as a sheet of writing paper and three times as long. Producing Chinese calligraphy with ink and brush required a great deal of skill, which my mother possessed. It became a part of the New Year ritual for my mother to write *duilian* for our neighbours, who would then each paste a long strip on each side of their front doors with a shorter strip above the door. *Duilian* is a type of scroll carrying messages of good luck and wishes of wealth, all in rhyme. Mother never seemed to turn anybody down and, every time neighbours came to ask, she would drop whatever she was doing and gladly oblige. As a child, I could not quite understand why she was so indiscriminately helpful. To do *duilian* for the Guans and Madam Jiao, our good neighbours, was one thing, but to do it for some other neighbours who were quite unfriendly to us since father's death was beyond my young comprehension. 'Mama, why do you do it for them?' I used to ask her in frustration, particularly when I saw the making of my new clothes yet again being interrupted. The New Year should be a time of goodwill, my mother used to say to me, with one of her indulgent smiles. Keen to do something different for each of our neighbours, my mother had been giving a lot of thought to the rhymes lately. To make things more complicated, she had to be extra careful this year, as she had been reprimanded the previous year by the party secretary of our residential committee for writing something that had relevance to wealth and good fortune, and could therefore have been interpreted as too materialistic or too feudalistic. 'Can you write just one character on this?' Madam Guan almost murmured, quite unusual for her. She had just come to ask my mother to write the Chinese character *fu*, meaning good fortune and blessing. 'I won't tell anybody you wrote it,' she said.

'It is upside-down,' I shouted as she was pasting it on her front door. 'What do you know, No. 4,' she resumed her loud voice, taking a pause from smoking her cigarette. 'Upside-down' sounded the same as 'arrive' in spoken Chinese, hence Madam Guan was playing on words. In Chinese, as in English, but more so, words that sound the same can be written totally differently and mean quite different things. This can be confusing but can also provide scope for endless puns. In Madam Guan's case, though the word pasted upside-down might be a little difficult to read, the fact of its being upside-down was a clear symbol of its intended meaning.

As a child, I was always excited about the New Year, which often seemed to take an eternity to arrive. I could not understand at that time why adults often said things like 'yet another new year', as if each new year came around really quickly. With the Spring Festival, I had a lot to be excited about, and it usually brought me some much-welcomed new clothes. Often they were made by my mother on her Parrot sewing machine. As the youngest, I almost always had to wear clothes that my sisters had grown out of. My enduring memory of corduroy was seeing Meiling try on a pretty yellow corduroy jacket that my mother had bought for her. I can still remember the velvety feel that it had, and the crystal buttons that looked as tempting as fruit sweets. I insisted on trying it on too, and I was in tears when my mother told me that I should let Meiling have it first. Looking back, I can see the sadness in my mother's eyes when she had to comfort me, but she simply could not afford to buy new clothes for all of us.

My new clothes were often dragged down on their first outing by the weight of goodies. It was the tradition in our city at that time for neighbours and friends to go around to each other's houses to deliver festival wishes. I used to love going around with my mother, largely, I have to admit, for the toasted sunflower seeds, pumpkin seeds, savoury broad beans cooked in five spices with a strong star anise flavour, walnuts, dates and sweets that we were offered at every house. It was customary for the hosts to fill the children's pockets with these goodies, hence the weight in my clothes. Madam Jiao always offered the best, and I was particularly fond of her peanuts, a small luxury in our city. She would place the nuts in a shiny glass bowl next to another pretty bowl filled with delicious dried persimmon pieces lightly dusted with white sugar.

Chinese New Year was always heralded by magnificent displays of fireworks over the People's Square at midnight. Watching the fireworks was a highlight in our city and we were lucky to live close to the square so we could have an amazing close-up view of this fantastic display, skilfully conducted by a company of soldiers. Like all the children in our neighbourhood, I stayed up to watch the display. 'Don't forget to wake me up,' I would often say to my mother, just in case I dozed off at the wrong time and missed the display. With the fireworks came the continuous banging of fire crackers popping out from every corner of the city. The fire crackers were supposed to chase away all the evil spirits.

Jiaozi is a festival food not to be missed. As with all Chinese festivals, food is an integral part of the celebrations. We always had *jiaozi*, the little dumplings I mentioned earlier, on New Year's Day, and that was what everyone did in our city at that time. Dumpling making normally started on New Year's Eve, and it was traditional for all the family to gather together to see the New Year in. Making dumplings was a sociable way to catch up with all the news and gossip, as everybody could participate, even the young children. Ground pork, mixed with finely chopped fresh ginger, garlic and spring onion and seasoned with salt and sesame oil, was the base for the filling. Beating an egg in, and mixing in some Chinese mushrooms, would give the filling an extra layer of flavour. Adding dried shrimps or, even better, some chopped prawns, would be a real luxury. Vegetables, finely chopped, would be added to the filling, with Chinese cabbage, celery or carrots being the most popular. I still remember the sounds of intense chopping coming out of every house in our neighbourhood, almost simultaneously, often accompanied by the sizzling sound of frying.

My eldest sister Jing, an expert in making dough, always insisted that the pastry, made with white flour and cold water, needed to be well rested to help it become pliable and elastic before being rolled out. Rolling out the small circular dumpling wrappings was no easy task and required considerable skill, particularly as it was often the case that the person rolling the pastry had to keep up with quite a few people who were simultaneously making the filled dumplings. Each small circular piece of pastry was the wrapping for an individual dumpling, not much bigger than a couple of bites. My mother taught me how to make dumplings when I was quite young, mostly to get me involved. Stuffing the meat and vegetable mixture into each pastry piece with a pair of chopsticks was easy enough, at least after some practice, but sealing the dumplings properly was difficult. 'That's one of yours again,' Yan, who was normally in charge of boiling the dumplings, used to say in frustration as she saw the wrappings and fillings coming apart in the boiling water. My dumplings, however, could often escape Yan's criticism if they were being fried or steamed. Dipped into some vinegar and spicy sauce mixed with a touch of ground garlic, the dumplings tasted wonderful, hot or cold.

Four Happiness looked divine. The four meatballs sat happily on a plate, with a piece of green Chinese long-leaf and slices of white bamboo shoots placed decoratively on top. Four Happiness, or four happy meatballs, is a traditional Chinese dish said to date back to the eighth century and to originate from Shandong, the home of Confucius. I once heard Madam Guan insisting, in a debate with another neighbour, that the four happiness represented good fortune, career success, longevity and marital bliss, while the other neighbour was adamant that they meant something else. Their heated debate only came to a end when Madam Jiao intervened by suggesting that the four happiness stood for affluence, health, harmony and joyfulness, which both Madam Guan and the other neighbour seemed to find difficult to argue with.

To cook this dish, my mother chopped a piece of lean pork almost as finely as if it had been minced. She then put the pork into a large mixing bowl before adding some finely chopped ginger and spring onion. Then, she beat a couple of eggs into the mixture before adding a splash of rice wine and a spoonful of cornflour. Seasoned with salt and soy sauce, the pork mixture was then carefully rolled into four balls, each the size of a table tennis ball. She then shallow-fried them briefly in a wok to give them a tint of gold colour before carefully transferring them on to a plate, ready for steaming. Four Happiness was always a delicious treat, which my mother often cooked on the Spring Festival or whenever there was a cause for celebration.

'You must have some of these phoenix feet; they are a real delicacy,' Madam Jiao sounded excited as she came in with a china plate with steam still rising from it. It was a plate of chicken feet, imaginatively named and neatly presented with a hint of star anise and oyster sauce that wafted through our house. 'It's good for the complexion and reduces wrinkles,' she said to my mother, with a twinkle in her eyes. She had come to thank my mother for the red paper scissors-cut my mother had done for her. She was particularly fond of the image of the plump boy riding on a big fish, she said. Being plump was good – after all, it meant good food and therefore affluence, while fish symbolised abundance. Chinese people love symbolism and like to play on words.

'Let's see who is the lucky one this year,' said Madam Guan as she took a coin out of her pocket. As always, she seemed to be able to find free time to come over and supervise us. In her mind, my mother, an engineering graduate, was perhaps too educated to be domesticated. Madam Guan wanted to put the coin inside one of our dumplings, and she believed, like many locals in our city at that time, that whoever had the dumpling with the coin in it would be immensely blessed for the year. Meiling and I giggled under our red lanterns as Madam Guan enthusiastically tried to bury the coin in the mixture. Luck, red, the sounds of chopping and sizzling, together with *jiaozi* and phoenix feet, all form a part of my vivid memories of the New Year celebrations. That year, I happened to be the lucky one.

6

Spiritual Food and the Courtyard House

Mr Liu, the newly arrived PE teacher, brought a breath of fresh air to our school. Not only was he a much-welcomed addition to the teaching staff who were all female, but he was also the first graduate our school had had for a very, very long time. He was not just any graduate, though, as he was once a worker-peasant-soldier student. A thin man in his late twenties, he looked impressed when I told him that I reckoned he had been a model worker before he was chosen to go to university. Amused, he smiled at me with his big expressive eyes, almost wondering how I knew about it.

Actually, I didn't know that much about it except what I had heard from my cousins and their friends. It seemed to be the case that, if you were a model worker, an excellent peasant or an outstanding soldier, you would have a good chance to be recommended by your superiors for a university place. Then the recommendation needed to be rubber stamped by a special committee. The special committee was a very powerful organisation, and rubber stamping was far more influential than it appeared. If you were lucky enough to get recommended and approved, then you would become a worker-peasant-soldier student. Studying Mao's thoughts was an integral part of the curriculum, although with an emphasis on practical rather than theoretical study. Becoming a worker-peasant-soldier student was quite a big thing. Apart from anything else, it was in fact quite difficult to get a university place, considering that many universities were being closed and that the university-entrance examination system had been abolished since the start of the

Cultural Revolution in 1966. I recall how my cousins once talked, enthusiastically and with a degree of envy, about a friend who got promoted fast after she had graduated from Inner Mongolia Industrial University. 'Aunt, it is all down to *guanxi*, the great connection,' I heard Jinmin, the keen photographer of our cousins' circle, complaining to my mother one day. Looking back, I can understand his cynicism better now. After all, he had twice been turned down by the special committee.

'Look at this book,' an excited Meiling showed us a collection of posters that Teacher Liu, as we called Mr Liu, had lent her. Having spotted her talent after seeing a watercolour she had done of a young girl working in a paddy field, Mr Liu put Meiling in charge of producing a poster for our school. Since his arrival, Mr Liu, apart from teaching arithmetic and PE, had set up an art group and the school's broadcasting station as well as a volleyball team. School became more fun and even some previously naughty children started behaving themselves, having found outlets for their energy in art and sports.

One day Meiling was absorbed in her painting as my mother was cooking lunch. Lunch was runner beans fried with Chinese mushrooms and garlic. I was given the job of preparing the beans. First, I topped each bean with two fingers, and then pared away the stringy edge on its seam before tailing it. After that, I broke the beans into thumb-length pieces before giving them a good wash. With the oil hot in the wok, my mother added the beans, gave them a good stir, and then added some Chinese mushrooms, hydrated and cut into thin strips. After another good stir, she added half a small bowl of boiled water to the wok and then put the lid on to leave the beans and mushrooms to cook for about six minutes. She then added two cloves of roughly chopped garlic to the wok and gave it another good stir before it was ready to be served.

Fried runner beans with Chinese mushrooms was one of our favourite vegetable dishes. The full-flavoured and rather chewy Chinese mushrooms made a welcome supplement to meat which we could only have occasionally. With lunch, my mother also boiled two salted eggs from our very own chicken. Preserving eggs in salt water was our way to make them last into the long winter months. In salted eggs, the egg yolk is the most delicious part, but it can be tricky to achieve a good yolky taste without getting the egg white too salty. I was particularly fond of the yolk, and my sister Yan would occasionally bribe me with her portion, so that I would do more washing-up. With a few pieces of my mother's delicious *laobing*, a type of Chinese pancake similar to pitta bread, lunch was simple but delightful.

It was not only Meiling who was busy at lunchtime. I was also busy trying to remember by heart the contents of a leader article in the *People's Daily*, a broadsheet and the official voice of the country at that time. An anti-Lin and anti-Confucius campaign was under way in the country and our school was certainly not to be left behind. Lin was one of Chairman Mao's former comrades turned opponent.

Since Mr Liu recruited me to his broadcasting team, I soon became the voice of the school radio, a highly coveted position which brought me friends and admirers. Every morning during the school term, rain or shine, I would pick up the key to the broadcasting room from the school gatekeeper at about 7.30, half an hour before classes started. The school gatekeeper was a pleasant retired man and every morning, when he saw me, he would smile at me from behind his pipe, his constant friend. The broadcasting room was a small narrow room with equipment neatly placed on the shelves by Mr Liu. Our few precious records were carefully put inside their sleeves and placed in a large drawer. Every day, I got the big black records out and then put them away with extreme care and great pride. Seated at the little desk from which I broadcast, I had a good view of the school playground where some pupils would do morning exercises while others performed their rota duty of classroom cleaning, all accompanied by the music and my reading. There were no cleaning ladies in our school, which was the norm in our city at that time. All the cleaning was done by pupils on a rota basis, including the cleaning of whatever glass was left. Often, between playing music and reading from books chosen by Mr Liu, I wolfed down my breakfast, normally pickles sandwiched between the two halves of a steamed bread. Sometimes, instead, I would have *mahua*, a deep-fried dough mixed with sugar, twisted into the shape of a flower and coated with sesame.

The highlight for me as the school's key broadcaster was at the school's sports events, which we held at the end of each of our two terms before we broke off for the Spring Festival and summer holiday. At each sports event, Mr Liu would set up a small canvas booth next to the rostrum, or the chairman's platform as we called it in our city. It made me feel rather important to sit near the VIP guests from the education department of the railway bureau and to read the contributions flowing in from different classes. The contributions were normally poems or slogans aimed at cheering on the contestants. In fact, competition was often as intense off the running tracks as on them. Some classes could get quite upset if they felt that their poems or slogans were not being given a good slot.

'Come on, come on, Class 2,' I cheered the 200-metre sprinters of my class at a sports event to mark International Children's Day on 1 June. On Children's Day every year our school, like all the schools in China, would hold some events to celebrate the day. My cheers from the broadcasting booth did wonders for the morale of the competitors of our class, and particularly for Zhu Liping who, to the astonishment of the audience, suddenly overtook the two front runners and leapt to the finishing line like a true star. I was not supposed to have done this and, in fact, I was soon told off by Teacher Liu for voicing support for my class so openly. 'Unfair to other classes,' he said quite seriously. I promised that I would not do this again, but I was secretly pleased that I had done so. The truth is that I did it for Zhu Liping, who had saved our bacon in the arithmetic relay I had nearly lost for our class earlier on. Not particularly good at sports, I had reluctantly entered the competition – in fact, I didn't have much choice in the matter as Mr Liu, keen to get as many pupils involved in the sports as possible, had put me forward. In our school, good pupils didn't say no to our teachers who were, generally speaking, not so keen on argumentative pupils. Besides, there was actually a good reason for Mr Liu to put me in the arithmetic relay, which involved five mixed teams with four runners in each team. Being good at mental arithmetic would compensate for me not being particularly a fast runner, since the relay involved each competitor running 100 metres and then solving an arithmetic problem. I can still remember clearly how I ran as fast as I could after the second team mate had passed me the baton, but was soon being left behind. Cheers of excitement erupted, I recall, as I came into the lead after speedily writing down the answer to an arithmetic question which was laid out on a small clipboard and placed on the track. The cheers turned into disappointed sighs when three fast runners, though much slower at solving their arithmetic questions, caught up and overtook me. Having received the baton from me, Zhu Liping, unfazed by our fourth position, took off at a tremendous speed. It was quite entertaining to watch him, with his big thick glasses held on with an elastic band and his famously large ears flapping like a pair of wings. There were loud cheers as he overtook first one, and then another two, after he jotted down, at supersonic speed, the answer to his arithmetic question. Then, like a star sprinter, he dashed to the finishing line and threw his hands in the air. I remember that I wanted to tell him what an amazing thing he had done in the arithmetic relay, but I didn't. I was a little shy and perhaps too embarrassed to do so.

I had first met Zhu Liping before we became classmates. It was a Sunday afternoon, and my mother, keen for us to do some sports, took us all to the sports ground of our school, a popular playground and sports venue in our neighbourhood. The new table-tennis tables there attracted some attention and there was a game under way, with a few onlookers. The three new tables, in fact not proper table-tennis tables, more like concrete platforms, built to last, were close to each other. After we had secured a vacant table, Jing and Yan put our net in the middle. Jing and Yan already played table tennis, which we always called ping-pong, and were quite good players. When my father was alive, our mother, a competent player who had represented the railway bureau in some national amateur competitions, used to take them out to practise. Yan's face was often like a barometer, and we could all tell, I remember, as soon as they came back, whether she had won or lost on any particular day. Jing always seemed to take her loss quite well, though she relished telling us how she 'slaughtered' Yan one day with her forehand smash, a new stroke she had learnt. Mother had never had much time to teach Meiling and me, however, and in any case, I probably didn't have the aptitude. As usual, my focus and priority in front of the new ping-pong table, was to choose the bat of the right colour. Choosing was not difficult, as we had only had two old bats, one porcelain blue and the other dark red.

Zhu Liping's father was warm and friendly, a stocky man in

his mid-forties who had recently relocated to the railway bureau in our city from near Shanghai. To Yan's delight, he seemed rather impressed by her ability to make forceful shots in her pen-holding style, a fashionable way of holding bats in China. He introduced himself as *Lao* Zhu, or Old Zhu to my mother, in a southern accent, similar to that of Uncle Deng, which I could tell my mother liked. In our city at that time, adults mostly addressed each other by their surnames, except among some close friends. Mr Zhu was not really old, *lao* was just a friendly term people used in front of surnames. As a child, I often found it a little confusing and somewhat fascinating why some people who appeared quite young had 'old' prefixing their surnames while people who appeared rather old had 'young' as a prefix. 'Well, it's all about the overall feel,' Jing once explained to me in a mysterious and adult-like way.

Mother introduced all her brood to a smiling Mr Zhu, and he in turn introduced his son whom he'd just been playing ping-pong with. I looked at Zhu Liping, a cheerful boy with big glasses and big ears to match, and felt a little sorry for him for being the only child, which was very unusual in our city at that time, when we were used to seeing families with three, four – or even eight children as in Madam Guan's household. A good ping-pong player, Mr Zhu needed little encouragement from the onlookers before asking my mother to have a game, which she gladly agreed to. It was a friendly game, and it was fun to see my mother enjoying herself with some pretty impressive shots, spins and smash.

It was a hot summer's day in 1974. The full-page leader article in the *People's Daily* came as a big challenge to me. Apart from its length, I struggled to understand the contents of the article, which was a wrapped-up (or sometimes not so wrapped-up) criticism of some of Mao's colleagues and critics. Confucius was even dragged out as a symbol of old feudal ideology 'which must be eradicated from our thoughts'. Confucian temples were under attack in parts of the country and some relics at Confucius's birthplace in Shandong were being destroyed, I overheard our neighbour Madam Jiao murmuring, quite secretly, to my mother one day. The school was putting on an exhibition with illustrated posters, which Meiling and her art group friends had been working on for quite a few days. As the voice of the school, I was the natural choice to guide the whole school through the exhibition by using the leader article as the basis of my talk. I was pleased to be chosen, but deeply worried about not being able to deliver. My mother came to my rescue, and she helped me break the article into different chunks to match different posters. By doing so, we clearly but not so obviously, missed out some rambling parts. 'You did it perfectly,' my mother told me after I had a much-needed snooze before embarking on my important task. Apparently, I had recited my talk during my sleep and it had come out very well.

'She sounded too soft and too sympathetic to that old rotten thing,' one of the older boys in our school burst out at the end of one of my talks. The boy, who was about 13, waved his finger at me and complained loudly to Mr Liu. Mr Liu listened in silence as the boy complained about me. To be accused of being sympathetic to Confucius and to feudal thoughts was a very serious matter, particularly as the accusation came from a boy whose father was the head of propaganda in the railway bureau, a powerful division in our city at that time. Mr Liu was aware of the consequences, and tried to handle the situation as delicately as possible. 'I'm sure she didn't mean to . . .' Mr Liu started. 'Who do you think you are, trying to protect a potential young anti-revolutionary?' the boy interrupted, turning his focus of attack straight on to Mr Liu. 'You of all people should know better, shame on you, a former worker-peasant-soldier student.' He became more excited as the crowd became bigger. He seemed to relish being in the spotlight, constantly pointing aggressively at Mr Liu and me.

The situation became highly charged, with the boy making all sorts of accusations, some of them fashionable and much used in our city at that time. Thinking about it now, he was quite articulate, perhaps a trait he had inherited from his father. 'Drop it,' came a voice from the back of the crowd. The boy, so carried away with himself, was not to be interrupted. To show his contempt, he spat in the direction of the voice while constantly waving his fingers towards Mr Liu and me, the focus of his attack. 'Drop it now,' the voice at the back became louder and more assertive. A dramatic pause followed, with the boy struggling, unusually, to find the right things to say. To cover up his loss of face, a really serious matter in our city, he tried to wave dismissively in the direction of the voice, but his face betrayed a rare sense of helplessness and defeat. People turned around in the direction of the voice and wondered who was behind this remarkable voice.

I knew the voice well and I knew as soon as I heard it that it would put an end to this farce. Jianping stood there, looking a little perplexed by the amazement shown by the crowd, and he blinked his small eyes as he brushed aside his fringe, something he did often. To be honest, I used to tease him a little for being too conscious of his image for a boy of nine. He was the younger brother of the boy who was shouting at me and Mr Liu.

Jianping sat next to me in class and was a fan of my broadcasting. Occasionally, I would allow him to come in to the broadcasting room for a quick look, a privilege not encouraged by Mr Liu. He often 'borrowed' my homework to copy, and in turn he would let me have any of his pretty yellow and red pencils from his well-stocked Panda pencil box. The colourful pencils were an attractive change from the dull grey pencils most of us had at that time. Jianping was very generous with his pencils, of which he seemed to have an endless supply from his father's office, but I had to be careful that my mother didn't see my new pencils, because every time she saw them she would ask me to return them. I was often in quite a quandary, and I even tried to argue with her on a couple of occasions, saying that I had earned the pencils by lending my homework to Jianping. My argument didn't seem to work, but my consolation was that at least I had the free use of whichever of Jianping's pencils I liked in school.

'Just go away,' Jianping's elder brother regained his calm a little. He waved his arm around a little in his effort to look authoritative, as an elder brother would do in our city at that time. 'No, you drop it,' Jianping said again. That sentence, said quite calmly but firmly, did the trick, and the elder brother left in a huff, spat in contempt and mumbled something like 'I'll sort you out later at home.' That was brave talk indeed, and he knew only too well that he could do nothing about his younger brother. The truth was that Jianping, as the youngest son, was the golden boy of the family and the apple of his parents' eyes. He could do no wrong.

My mother was pleased when I showed interest in playing violin, but she said apologetically that I would have to wait a while for her to save enough money to buy a violin. I nodded, trying to hide my disappointment, which I didn't do very successfully.

'Don't worry, we will soon save enough with your uncle's money,' she comforted me, deliberately sounding optimistic. Since my father's death, my uncle, my mother's brother, had been sending us money every month, as my mother's salary was barely enough for us to live on. 'Sorry, no post today,' our lively postman would sound very apologetic every time he had to break the news to us about the postal order we eagerly waited for. Sometimes, he would tease us, though, by pretending that he had no post as he passed us, only to turn up a moment later, magically producing the precious green envelope. To send money at that time, every month, after he had been paid, my uncle had to take money to a post office in Tianjin, where he lived. He would pay a handling fee and then the money would be in the system. Typically, after a week or so, we would receive a form in the post, which we would then take to a post office in our city; there we had to show our *hukou*, a residence registration document, and a proof of ID; then, at last, and we could withdraw the cash, normally about 20 yuan. That was quite a significant sum, considering it was about a fifth of my uncle's monthly salary and a third of my mother's. I can still feel, so many years later, the thin green envelope and see my uncle's brilliant writing in his blue fountain pen. Every time I think of this magical green envelope, my memories take me back to a butcher's in a small alley with a heavy beaded screen hanging in front of its main door. The screen was there to stop eager houseflies and other insects from savouring the food in the shop, so I was told by the shop owner. The shop mostly sold offal and it was extremely popular, partly because we didn't need to use any ration coupons there and partly because it was relatively cheap. It was not so long ago since the shop owner, a Mr Gong, started to stock pig trotters, very popular but in very short supply, thanks to some *guanxi*, I overheard him telling somebody.

Getting the hair off the trotters was the first step towards a delicious dish. Using a cast-iron poker heated in our stove until it was red hot, my mother burned off the hair, a slightly messy process. Washing the trotters and cutting them into halves, she then put them into a saucepan of boiling water. After leaving them on the boil for a few minutes, she would take the trotters out, drain them and rinse them again. She heated some sesame oil in the wok before adding a generous amount of crystal sugar, and waited until the sugar melted. She then put in some Chinese peppercorns and star anise, which would give out a nice fragrance, before adding some roughly chopped ginger and spring onion, rice wine, soy sauce and finally the trotters. A good stir later, she poured some boiled water into the wok, just below the level of the trotters, brought it to the boil and then added salt. Then she let the trotters simmer on a low heat until they were tender and cooked, and finally she brought them to the boil once again before serving. The tender trotters, braised in the sauce, were delicious. They were also reputed to be good for the skin, and the thought of having a beautiful complexion after eating the trotters added yet another dimension to our enjoyment.

Even the pigs' toes could provide hours of entertainment in a game that was popular, mostly with girls. It involved five to nine pig-toe bones and required good coordination and dexterity. The basic idea of the game was to throw one bone into the air, and the others on to the ground, and to make a pattern out of the ones on the ground whilst the first bone, or the 'lead' one, as we called it, was still airborne. It could be tricky to start with, and I still remember the first time I played the game. After I threw the lead toe in the air, I could barely catch it again, let alone gather the remaining four toes all with the same hand, which my more experienced friend Fei seemed to be able to do effortlessly, even with nine toes. She was very good at the game, and from the way she threw her lead toe high in the air, you could tell she was proud of her skills and sometimes liked to show off, particularly when there were onlookers. After she threw her lead toe in the air, with some considerable flair, she would sometimes use her right index finger and middle finger as if they were a pair of chopsticks, to turn all the toes to stand on their fronts, or sides, or in a certain pattern. All this manoeuvring was done while the lead toe was in the air and then, when she caught the lead toe, she would again throw it in the air and repeat the manoeuvre, albeit even more daringly and elaborately. She made it look so easy.

It was a friendly and flexible game, and normally there were two or three players in a game. Some girls in the neighbourhood used to spend hours playing it either with friends or on their own. Apart from the game itself, the girls would often compare the toes in their possession with those that their friends had. On top of being a good player, Fei, a tall girl with a rounded face and perpetually red cheeks, was also the proud owner of a good collection of pig toes and lamb toes. Pig toes were good, and lamb toes were better, as they were more dainty and more regular than their porcine counterparts. They were not easy to collect, as one needed to go through quite a few trotters or lamb legs to accumulate enough good toes. Because of the rationing, it could be a mammoth task, which I found too daunting even to venture into. Fei had a secret weapon, because her mother worked in a meat shop which was famous for its cooked pig trotters and lamb leg. Her collection was, unsurprisingly, rather large, and I remember seeing some toes in her collection painted very creatively in some quite dazzling colours.

'Where are all my pig toes?' I asked my mother one afternoon after school, frustrated that my set of five pig toes, all carefully cleaned and beautifully painted in red, seemed to have disappeared from where I had left them. I had done most of my homework, and thought I would just practise for a while the new trick Fei had shown me during one of the breaks earlier on. Mother looked at me sympathetically but apart from shaking her head gently, she did not say much and did not, quite uncharacteristically, offer to help find them either. Having searched around the house for a while, I finally gave up, quite convinced, to my greatest annoyance, that I had left them behind somewhere by accident. My frustration and annoyance were partly because I had lost something that I had enjoyed playing with, but largely because I did not want to upset Fei. It was not so long ago that Fei, one of the very few classmates who had stood up for me in front of the school bullies, had finally decided, after some really careful consideration, to give those toes to me.

Encouraged by my interest in the violin, my mother started to teach me to read music. 'All this spiritual food stuff is a waste of time,' I heard Madam Guan talking to Madam Jiao one day as I was practising singing the music notes of a revolutionary song. I had just had my first music theory lesson from my mother, who used a chopstick as a baton. Madam Guan, excellent at multi-tasking, was talking to Madam Jiao between cooking and trying to repair a grater, the 'wretched thing' she had just broken. It was difficult to miss Madam Guan's loud and throaty voice and in fact, I would go as far as to say that our neighbourhood would feel a little strange without her presence being felt. She was going to cook 'three shredded vegetables' for supper with the fresh potato, carrot and green pepper Mr Guan brought back from the railway bureau's farm where he was a supervisor.

'That poor child, she's better off learning to cook,' Madam

Guan announced firmly. I was intrigued by their conversation and stopped to listen in. 'Cooking could at least help her to get a job, say, working in a canteen somewhere,' she continued between occasional puffs on her cigarette. 'She is a bit naïve,' she went on, referring now to my mother. Apart from nodding and sighing occasionally, Madam Jiao didn't say much. Aware of my attention, she cleared her throat a little to remind Madam Guan that I was in earshot. But Madam Guan was not the one to hold back and continued her monologue. She looked a little uneasy for a moment, as she caught my eye, but she soon resumed in her normal way. Thinking about it, Madam Guan actually had a good point, as there were indeed many canteens in our city at that time, and many employers provided canteen food, mostly at a subsidised price, to their employees. Guan No. 3 worked in one of the railway bureau's canteens and seemed to be very happy with her job there. Sometimes she liked to show off the large, white buns she brought home from her canteen.

The long train, with its steam engine, took us on the 14-hour journey overnight to Beijing. Our carriage was full. It was always this busy, my mother explained to Meiling and me, as trains were the main and often the only means of transport for such a journey then. Like Meiling, I found it difficult to get any sleep, and the thrill of being on such a long journey and seeing Beijing, both for the first time, was simply too exciting for both of us.

Beijing greeted us with a brilliant sunny day. 'The White Pagoda, look, look!' Meiling jumped up, with her hands still wet from feeding a pair of Mandarin ducks on the lake. 'We're here,' she squeaked in excitement. Looking up, in front of me I saw the famous white pagoda for the first time. It stood graciously amid lush green trees and the yellow glazed tiles of the nearby old buildings, gracefully bearing the marks of its hundred years of history. We were near the Beihai park, not far from the Forbidden City, and it felt almost surreal to see the White Pagoda and the Forbidden City in real life for the first time. I felt that I knew them so well because I had seen them so many times in prints and pictures, yet it was our first actual encounter. Meiling and I were overwhelmed – we had not yet got over our earlier excitement at seeing Tiananmen Square for the first time, which we had drawn many times before in art class.

We were in Beijing with my mother, to visit our grandfather. Mother had not been to Beijing for some years now. Although she had managed to obtain a free return ticket for herself, an occasional perk for employees of the railway station, she could not afford to take all four of us with her so she decided to take her two younger daughters. In any case, Jing and Yan were old enough to look after themselves, and Madam Guan had promised to keep an eye on them.

'Tanghulu,' came a clear voice accompanied by the equally clear ringing of a bicycle bell. On the front bar of the bicycle of the vendor selling tanghulu or sugar gourds, was a colourful display of sugar-glazed hawthorn fruits on sticks, neatly arranged in a bamboo basket. The small red haws, glazed in caramelised sugar, usually five on a stick, looked like gourds in shape, hence the name, and were delicious to eat, with the sugar beautifully complementing the sharp taste of the fruit. 'Ninhao,' the vendor, a trim middle-aged lady, said hello to my mother politely as she lifted the muslin from over the sugar gourds. Meiling and I smiled at each other, a little amused by her way of greeting, very different from 'chilema,' literally 'have you eaten?' the most common form of greeting in our city at that time. Even when a small number of people said hello, often considered highly sophisticated in our neighbourhood, they would mostly use *nihao* rather than *ninhao*, the difference in usage being similar to that between 'tu' and 'vous' in French. I had had sugar gourd in our city before, but somehow having this famous Beijing snack in its place of origin added an extra layer of taste to this delightful and more-ish snack.

Walking into the courtyard house deep in the *hutong*, an old narrow alley in Beijing, was like walking into a classic Chinese story. A big stone step, a pair of double wooden gates and another half-moon gate later, we were in a sunny courtyard with lilac and pomegranate trees beautifully framing the one-storey courtyard house. '*Ninhao*,' a parrot greeted us from a cage under the trees, distracting me momentarily from gazing at the attractive verandas interlinking the rooms on all sides of the courtyard. This courtyard house, my mother told us, was originally built for one family, to accommodate several generations to live under the same roof. 'Such a big house for just one family,' I marvelled. 'Not any more,' she explained. Like nearly all traditional courtyard houses, this one had been divided into different dwellings and every one was now occupied by a different family. I remember that I was quite disappointed with her reply, and I suppose, in a way, it took away from me a little bit of the romance of the house. Thinking about it now, the arrangement was somewhat similar to having a large Victorian family house converted into separate flats.

We were a little overwhelmed by the friendly neighbours, and many of them greeted us like old friends. 'Let's get the guests some tea,' said an old man who stopped feeding his goldfish to gesture in the direction of his home of two sunny rooms. It didn't take long for his daughter, a plump lady, to give us each a cup of jasmine tea. Our tea drinking was accompanied

by the old man's running commentary on all the nine house-
holds in the courtyard. As it was close to lunchtime, more people
were coming home, which in turn made the introduction process
last longer, with almost everybody keen to tell Meiling and me
a bit about their *hutong* and about Beijing, once they found out
that it was our first trip. It was a picture of harmony. Looking
back, I think it incredible for all the families in the courtyard
to mange to get on with each other within such a tight space.
Glorious as the courtyard house was, it was pretty cramped and
crowded with so many families now sharing the space originally intended for one family. But I suppose that they only made
the most of what they had, which was the norm then.

My grandfather was a thin, gentle man with big brown eyes
and a goatee beard. Being frail and a little unwell did nothing
to distract him from being attentive to Meiling and me. He took
out a pretty blue tin from under the bed that was tucked into
a corner of his room, part of the courtyard house. A delicate
fragrance came out of this airtight cake tin, as he opened it to
offer us the beautiful cakes. I was instantly taken by the deli-
cious-looking flaky pastry, and especially by the cake with a red
rose pattern stamped on top. It tasted just as exquisite as it
looked, and the rose petal paste with a touch of sesame inside
the pastry was simply extraordinary. To Meiling and me, whose
cake experience was mostly of either the over-oily or over-dry
cakes of our city, this was an eye opener. These were an absolute
delight and a true luxury.

Grandfather was a learned man who many years ago had
attended Qinghua University, the Chinese equivalent of Oxford
or Cambridge. He looked serene, sitting on an old-fashioned
elm chair with an exquisite carving on the back, one of the very
few pieces of his old furniture that had survived the wars and
the Red Guards. I can still smell the smell of this old chair

mixed with a hint of mould and the scent of grandfather's lilac soap. 'They will enrich your life,' he said encouragingly about the art and music learning that Meiling and I told him about, while we were tucking into the delicious cakes. I am not sure whether at that time I fully understood the deep meaning he conveyed about music and art, but I remember that his words certainly made me feel good. Grandfather's encouragement was as pleasing to the senses as the cakes he had bought specially for us, particularly after what Madam Guan had said to Madam Jiao about spiritual food.

'Do you want to buy a couple of *liang* of minced pork today?' came the voice of a neighbour, whose silhouette we could see through the paper pane of grandfather's window. He was on his way to a nearby shop to buy some meat for lunch and offered to pick up a couple of *liang*, approximately 100 grams, of minced pork for us, as he thought my grandfather might like us to have a popular Beijing dish. I could not believe my ears. So was it true that they could buy meat just like that in Beijing, so casually and so easily? My eyes must have betrayed my surprise and amazement, and my grandfather nodded, with a smile, as if he had read my mind. That was a mini culture shock to me; after all, the meat-buying I knew was always linked to ration vouchers and long queues.

My mother heated a wok over my grandfather's stove, which was burning merrily with honeycomb briquettes, rarely seen in our home city. Putting in a generous amount of oil, she stirred in the fresh minced pork, adding finely chopped ginger and spring onions. She kept stirring until a distinct fragrance emerged. In the meantime, she mixed together a generous amount of thick soy bean sauce and plum sauce with cold water and blended the mixture thoroughly with a pair of chopsticks until it had the consistency of single cream. Adding the sauce mixture into the wok, she stirred constantly until it came to the boil before splashing in a touch of seasoning. Leaving the mince to simmer in the sauce for a few more minutes, my mother boiled the noodles also brought back by the helpful neighbour. Rinsing the noodles briefly with cold water in a colander, she then transferred them, with a pair of chopsticks, into our china bowls. With some pre-prepared cucumber slices, bean sprouts and blanched spinach, the noodles with the meat sauce, an old favourite with Beijingers, made a delightful meal.

'Goodbye to the capital,' came the announcement on the train as it left the platform of Beijing station, leaving behind the crowd waving their goodbyes to their relatives and friends. The early evening sun shone on us as we travelled home westwards. I was sad to leave Beijing, and even the cakes that my grandfather had given us didn't seem to be enough to take away my blue feeling. It felt as if I had left something behind, and it was something I found difficult to fathom out. Then I realised what it was – I had left my heart behind, and, from then on, I longed to return.

7

Brain Food and the Angry Dragon

A loud bang burst out and a crowd, consisting mostly of children, shrieked in excitement while covering their ears with their hands. A brief silence followed, replaced by yet more sounds of joy as puffed sweetcorn came out of a canvas tube attached to an oval-shaped cast-iron roaster. A stocky man in his forties, looking relieved at the crowd's reaction, put the popcorn into an aluminium container and passed it on to a boy of eight or nine, who in turn paid him the equivalent of a few pence. The man then assembled the canvas tube and filled his roaster with another portion of sweetcorn from another person in the crowd. There should have been a queue, but we were not into orderly queues in our city at that time. The man took a big mouthful of tea from his heavily stained glass jar, wiped some black coal dust from his face with his sleeve, and went straight back to drawing his bellows and rotating the roaster over a red-hot coal stove.

This was our popcorn man and he was a frequent visitor to our neighbourhood. With graded grains, refined flour and scented white rice being a luxury, our staple food consisted of mostly roughage. We had sweetcorn on the cob, boiled sweetcorn 'rice', ground sweetcorn wire noodles, sweetcorn buns with dates, boiled red sorghum, red sorghum buns with kidney beans, millet soup, ground millet buns, and so the list goes on. In spite of my mother's creativity, sometimes even she had to admit defeat. The truth was that we were just tired of the roughage, no matter how it was wrapped up, and the old saying that even the best housewife would struggle to cook without rice became more of a reality than a metaphor. The arrival of the popcorn man was therefore warmly welcomed by children as well as by their parents, who were just pleased to see the appeal that the puffed sweetcorn and red sorghum had created.

'The Red Flag was red because of the blood of our heroes,' a proud Little Red Guard recited his well rehearsed speech in the bright April sun. We, the whole school, were standing in front of the monument to Heroes of the People in the People's Park, the main park in our city at that time. It was *Qingming*, the traditional tomb sweeping day, a day which Chinese people had marked for centuries, combining remembering the dead with celebrating life and growth in spring. Every year on this day, all the schools in our city would organise an event to remember the people who had given their lives for the People's Republic.

Apart from the tomb sweeping, our school would normally organise some other activities, such as a tug-of-war, traditionally a popular sport for this day. Most of my class, including myself, became excited quite a few days beforehand and talked about our outing and picnics in some considerable detail. In fact, our picnics were nothing more than boiled eggs, steamed buns, pickles, fruit and possibly some sweets; but somehow, the bright spring weather seemed to add magic to them, and even a Fortnum & Mason hamper would probably have struggled hard to compete.

Every *Qingming*, my mother would cut from our trees some branches with new shoots on and carefully arrange them in my father's favourite vase. She would then place the vase in front of a framed photograph of my father. We had rarely talked about my father since his death, as if talking about him were like admitting that he was no longer with us. Acknowledging his absence was something we were all unwilling to do, and the easiest thing for us at that time, it seemed, was just to carry on.

'Fancy coming to have a look at my new picture books?' Jianping came to entice me once again with his new acquisition. With his father being the propaganda chief of the railway bureau, Jianping seemed to have an endless supply of picture books and always had new ones before anybody else. I shook my head while continuing to put coal into a white aluminium bucket. Surprised by my unusual lack of enthusiasm, he tried again. 'From Beijing, you know.' His small eyes blinked as I looked up from the pile of coal, or rather coal dust, that the coal man had just delivered on a mule cart. I shook my head again while looking admiringly at the big shiny lumps of coal in Madam Jiao's pile, which the coal man had insisted had been distributed randomly. I was now old enough to know that 'random' reflected Madam Jiao's good *guanxi*, and I soon gave up after some failed attempts at persuasion coupled with unsuccessful protests to the coal man. The prospect of making yet more coal balls, of coal dust mixed with yellow mud and water for easy burning, and the reality of having a smoke-filled house, didn't fill me with any joy at all. Deep down, I knew that I wished that my father were there.

Jianping was quick to spot the problem. 'Give her some big lumps,' he demanded, putting my bucket in front of the coal man. Rather taken aback but a little amused, the coal man asked who the hell Jianping thought he was. Unfazed, Jianping swept aside his fringe and started to take big lumps of coal off the cart, promptly stopped by another coal man who raised his whip. Madam Jiao quickly pulled the coal man back just in time to stop the whipping. 'Have some of my coal,' she said as she put some big lumps into my white bucket, now in Jianping's hands. She smiled and tried to pacify him by stroking him on his shoulders. 'You, wait, my father will sort you out,' a shocked Jianping shouted at the coal man who by now looked really sheepish after a well-informed Madam Guan told him that he had just upset the 'young emperor of our neighbourhood'. Looking back, as privileged as he was because of his father's position, the norm in our city at that time, Jianping was really a very fair and decent person. I wished that I had told him that he was my hero that day.

Jianping's family house, as expected, was much more spacious than ours. Looking me up and down, as if she were looking at a child bride, was a small old lady, probably in her seventies. Her curiosity was intense, and she looked as though she was oblivious of the fact that the child bride was something of the distant past. She was Jianping's grandmother. She was sitting on the *kang*, the warm brick bed. It was quite common for old people in our city at that time to sit on the *kang* during the day, and she was sewing. Eventually she managed to crack a smile as she continued with her sewing. In a blue cotton Chinese jacket and black trousers, she looked smart, with her thin hair tied neatly into a bun at the back of her head. I smiled at her, as I looked at the eye-catching Chinese buttons, elaborately made, on her jacket, but my eyes stopped at her small, pointed shoes.

I can still remember the sad look in her face as she realised why I was staring. Like Granny Wang, an old nanny my parents had hired when I was very small, Jianping's grandmother had had her feet bound when she was a young girl, which was considered a must at that time for a girl who otherwise would not find a husband. I had a faint memory of waking up one night and finding, in dim candle light, Granny Wang unwrapping a long white cloth from around her feet. Next to an enamel washing bowl were the small, three-inch-long cotton shoes that I had never seen her take off, not even when she slept. Almost as though she were conducting a ritual, Granny Wang put her small, pale feet into the bowl and sighed as she tipped her head back. The next thing I remember was her wrapping the cloth around her feet and ankles, stopping occasionally with sighs. I had almost forgotten about Granny Wang's bound feet until now and in fact, I had sometimes wondered whether it had all been part of a dream. Thinking about it now, I recall how I felt much blessed for living at a time when the practice of foot binding had long gone. I started to feel bad for staring at Jianping's grandmother. 'It's all right, little one,' the old lady said to alleviate my embarrassment.

'Have a little *jineijin*.' She offered me a tiny piece of a yellowish dried membrane which had just been cooked. I didn't like the look of it, and knew that it was basically the membrane lining of a chicken's stomach, but I didn't like to turn the old lady down, especially not after my indiscretion of staring at her feet. Besides, it was supposed to be quite a delicacy and as usual, it was considered highly nutritious. Indeed, *jineijin* was also used in traditional Chinese medicine as a remedy for indigestion and other stomach problems. I had heard this from Madam Jiao who was rather knowledgeable about this sort of thing.

With some tips from Jianping's mother, my mother found a butcher's shop affiliated to the railway bureau where she could buy more offal. It sounds laughable to think now that, with nearly everything we ate at that time, there was always a health benefit attached to it. But I suppose that might have been, to a large extent, our way of looking on the bright side and coping with the food shortages.

'That will be good for your brain.' The thin man coughed a little behind the meat counter. He sounded convincing enough, if only it had not been for his cough, which betrayed a little discomfort. As he pushed up his big glasses with the back of his left hand, he explained that the remaining pig's trotters, pig liver and *jineijin*, and so on – the more desirable items – were all reserved for the work units, a coded expression meaning that he was keeping them for people with *guanxi*. 'You can have either pig brain or sheep brain,' he said bullishly, as if the world were our oyster. I had a fit of giggles as he repeated the words 'pig brain', because in our city at that time, 'pig brain' was a derogatory term used to refer to someone who was very stupid and stubborn. Thinking about it now, this seems terribly unfair to the good old pig, which was not only a very clever animal but also contributed greatly to our diet with almost every part of its body.

'You will be even brighter after this,' he said to me with some relief, after my mother had chosen the pig brain without making any fuss. 'I can tell from your forehead,' he said mysteriously, and then, making sure that nobody was within earshot, he murmured with a little smirk, 'I'm a fortune teller, you know.' I didn't react, as I didn't really know how to. Quite a few people in our neighbourhood, I was told, believed in fortune telling at that time, but nobody dared to admit it for fear of being criticised as feudalistic or even anti-revolutionary. The smirk disappeared quickly before an expression of regret took over. 'You won't tell anybody, will you, clever little girl?' he said tensely, and the intensity of his expression frightened me a little. I nodded vigorously, desperate to end this interaction. My mother was very taken aback by this episode and she took me out of the shop as soon as the man had finished wrapping the pig brain in a piece of newspaper. 'Your change,' he shouted after us. Mother hesitated a little before she turned around and picked up the money, trying to avoid any eye contact with him. On the way home, she bought me half a dozen of my favourite milk and peanut toffees, perhaps to take away the unpleasant aftertaste of the experience at the butcher's.

The pig brain, which was quite delicate, was carefully rinsed with cold water before being put on to a piece of muslin over a bamboo steamer. Once it had been steamed, it was served with the usual mixture with soy sauce, finely chopped ginger and spring onions and a splash of sesame oil, salt and pepper. My mother used a strong fermented bean curd as a condiment, with a salty and intense flavour.

My long-awaited violin arrived at last, thanks to my generous uncle. With the arrival of the violin, I also acquired a violin teacher. My violin teacher Jiang was a handsome twenty-year-old soldier, and his mother Madam Wu, a biology teacher in No. 1 Middle School, had volunteered his tuition to me for free when she learnt about my interest in the violin. Madam Wu, a plump and extremely kind lady, was all smiles when my mother took me to see my teacher for the first time at their small but very tidy house, not far from ours. Taking a tin of sweets out of a bamboo basket, she offered me a couple of sweets, much to my delight. Although it was customary to be offered sweets during the Spring Festival, it was only seldom that one was offered them at any other time of year and so it was a real treat.

Jiang had just come home on holiday from the army where he flourished. He was recently commended on the Army's Day, Madam Wu told us proudly, because his musical talents enriched the life of his fellow soldiers. I remembered how, when I was much younger, I used to look adoringly at him as he fooled around with his brother, a trumpet in his hand, blowing out a melody from time to time. My lessons started with the basics and, all through his holiday, Jiang religiously gave his time to teach me and supervise my practice. Then the time came for him to return to the army, and I was sad to lose my teacher, who promised to come back to teach me on his next holiday. During his absence, I practised hard. Thinking about it now, part of the reason that I practised so hard then was to impress him on his return, so that he would continue to teach me.

My mother was pleased with my progress, but was particularly encouraged when Jiang told her that the army was recruiting soldiers with special talents in the arts. Jiang's inside information prompted her to approach the residential committee of our neighbourhood about the possibility of my sister Yan, soon to be 15 years old, joining the army, and her hopes were a little dashed when Madam Wang, the leader of the committee, a thin middle-aged woman with short hair, told her that there were already many applicants in the queue. Joining the army was a very popular move in our city at that time, and, apart from the glory of being in the army, it provided good job prospects, which were then in very short supply. My mother went to talk to Auntie Song, hoping to get some advice and, possibly, help, from her chief army representative husband. 'Getting into the quota is like getting gold dust,' Auntie Song told my mother authoritatively about the quota system which was supposed to ensure a fair allocation of limited opportunities. Auntie Song was in a position to know, as she had only recently secured two places for her two older sons. 'I'll see what I can do,' she told my mother with a sigh that betrayed a lack of hope.

Even my mother, an optimist by nature, started to feel despondent at the lack of employment prospects for Jing and Yan, particularly Jing who at the age of 18, would soon finish her middle-school education. I remember catching my mother smoking a cigarette one day when I came back from school unexpectedly early. With her back facing the front door, which was open, she lit a cigarette from a pack she had prepared for guests, which was considered the polite thing to do in our city at that time. She drew a mouthful of smoke from the cigarette and immediately started to cough, obviously unable to cope with the smoke. I had never seen her smoke before, and in fact I would go as far as to say that she hated smoking. At first, she didn't notice my presence and continued smoking in spite of her cough. Then, as if she had suddenly realised something, she stubbed out the cigarette and put it away very quickly, almost as though she was hiding it. She then turned around with a faint smile, conveying a mixture of guilt and helplessness.

Our house was less lively now without my cousins and their friends, who had mostly returned to their home towns. I remember that it all seemed to happen quite quickly, and cousin Dong once mentioned something like a policy change. I didn't fully understand what was happening but I could see in their faces a sense of happiness and relief. It seemed to me that they could hardly wait to leave behind the so-called cultural re-education in this remote area of ours. I can still remember the excitement when Dong and her brother Shengli finally received, after a long and anxious wait, the confirmation that they would become worker-peasant-soldier students. They were lucky to have secured university places, considering that only a small number of universities were taking students at that time. Most universities were closed and, even with the few that were open, there was no proper entrance exam, and in most cases it came down to connections. In our city, it was almost impossible for fresh school leavers like Jing and Yan to get places at university, and so the future looked bleak for them.

To the sound of drums and cymbals, another criticism meeting was under way in our neighbourhood, led by a few Red Guards and their activist supporters. A group of onlookers had gathered near the convenience shop where I had gone to buy candles. Lately we had had a lot of power cuts, and the fear of more earthquakes following the catastrophic July 1976 earthquake in Tangshan, a city east of Beijing, seemed to have made the situation worse. Although only tremors were felt in our city when the quake hit Tangshan, people were nervous that we might not be so lucky with aftershocks. Our residential committee had organised some earthquake practice and had warned all residents of the danger of staying indoors in the event of any ground movement. A siren would sound, we were told, at the time of emergency, and people should immediately run to the identified safe areas. Amid all this, the criticism meetings, very much a frequent occurrence in our city at that time, carried on regardless. My mother always discouraged us from even watching such events. It was better to keep our heads down, she said. I could not avoid seeing it this time, and, like all the other onlookers, I was intrigued to see who would be the target of the criticism, the person in the dunce's cap. In the middle of a circle formed by activists and onlookers was a thin man standing uncomfortably on a wooden stool, with his big glasses protruding from under the dunce's cap. 'Down with the antirevolutionary,' a Red Guard shouted and raised her right arm, grabbing the man by his collar with her left hand and pulling him roughly down from the stool. I could not believe my eyes when I saw that the man in the dunce's cap was the pig-brain man, the self-proclaimed fortune teller. I bent my head down as soon as I recognised him and looked elsewhere, desperate to avoid catching his eyes. On reflection, I know, it was silly of me to think that he could have picked me out from a crowd just like that. Even if he could have, what was I frightened of? Was I frightened that he might have thought that I had betrayed his confidence, or was I frightened that people might link me to him? Head down, I walked away as quickly as I could, with the candles I had bought shaking wildly in my hands. It is easy to recognise now that my reaction was totally irrational, but we were living in an irrational time.

At least the enjoyment of food was not irrational, and not long after this incident, *wuxiang* beef, beef of five fragrances, was to cheer us up. One lovely autumn day, that coincided with her pay day, my mother bought half a kilo of beef. Washed and cut into cubes, the beef was marinated. Mother first ground some ginger, using a pestle and mortar, then she mixed the ground ginger with some ground fennel seeds, chopped spring onions, adding soy sauce, rice wine, sugar, salt, star anise, cloves and cassia bark to the marinade. After half a day or so of marinating, she transferred the beef together with the sauce into a wok, brought it to boil on high heat, and then left it to simmer until it was cooked. True to its name, *wuxiang* beef had many layers of fragrance and flavours, and was truly an excellent dish.

'What on earth are we going to do?' Madam Guan was howling uncontrollably over the fence while my mother, also sobbing, was trying to comfort her. I stared at them, not sure what was going on. 'What are you staring at?' my mother said to me impatiently, which was quite uncharacteristic of her. I had done nothing wrong and frankly I had no idea what was wrong.

The funeral music that played on my father's Panda radio said it all. 'Our great leader Chairman Mao has just passed away on this day, the 9th of September 1976,' came the solemn voice on the central broadcasting station. The announcement was followed by funeral music and then by yet more announcements. The whole country was in a state of shock.

In the days that followed, a sense of loss was felt in our neighbourhood, with adults talking in tears and children told to behave well to show respect. Behind the tears, there was an underlying fear and a great deal of uncertainty, apparent to all yet spoken by none. The truth was that nobody knew what lay ahead, and the 10-year-long Cultural Revolution seemed to have disabled people's ability to think optimistically.

Madam Jiao was as organised as ever. She got some black armbands from her department in the railway bureau, now in full swing preparing for various mourning events to pay tribute to our late leader. She was in tears as she handed some to my mother. 'Why, heavenly god and why now?' Madam Guan's sorrow was once again triggered by the sight of Madam Jiao's armbands. 'First we lost our dear Premier Zhou, then Chief Commander Zhu, then the dreaded earthquake, and now this,' she went on, crying continuously, only interrupting herself to cough.

'It's the angry dragon, isn't it?' Madam Guan said firmly as she lit a cigarette after a very long break, unprecedented on any other day. 'I thought I heard this year of dragon would be a difficult one,' she continued, the cigarette seeming to have calmed her down a little. But, taking a deep drag on it, she was on the verge of crying again. 'I never thought it would be so turbulent,' she said, fighting back her tears. As much as she believed in noodles and their aid to a smooth journey to heaven, Madam Guan was not in the mood to make any that day. In fact, she didn't seem to be in a fit mood to go anywhere near the kitchen.

8

The Iron Rice Bowl

Sanzi, bite-size pieces of pastry made into a pretty shape, were quite delicious to finish lunch with. Mixing pastry to a smooth and elastic dough with white flour, a generous amount of sugar, a teaspoon of vegetable oil and warm water, my mother rolled it out very thinly on a floured chopping board. She made it look easy, but my sister Jing had told me that it required quite a skill to make this paper-thin pastry, similar to filo pastry. Mother then cut out each *sanzi*, and coated them with sesame seeds. All done, she then deep-fried them in a wok. Although we didn't normally have sweet things to finish our meals with, the crispy and delicious *sanzi* were a welcome addition to our lunch of fried bean curd and boiled millet.

My mother was going to give up her iron rice bowl. To be precise, she was thinking about it, she told Meiling and me one lunchtime. It was a very big thing to give up a permanent job, the iron rice bowl that was meant to be there for life. She sounded a little awkward when she told us about this, constantly picking up her chopsticks and putting them down again. She looked as if she were expecting some sort of reaction from us, but appeared relieved when neither of us read too much into it.

Mother had lately started to talk about her job a little, and I seem to recall that there was some talk of a new manager, Mr Du, a fastidious person who liked to pick bones from eggs, as we described this type of fault-finding person in our city. Mother always seemed to take the flak for anything which went wrong in their team, as Mr Du was careful not to upset Auntie

Song and another colleague whose husband was also influential in the railway bureau. Although barely using her engineering background, my mother was, generally speaking, quite happy with her job in the team responsible for handling important documents and lost luggage claims. After all, this was considered to be a good place to be and only well-connected people such as Auntie Song could get into it. Besides, working here gave her the flexibility to work shifts so that she could spend more time with us and have more time to cook. The residential committee of our neighbourhood had not come back with any good news about Yan joining the army. The fact of the matter was that the number of people wanting a place far exceeded the number of opportunities available. My mother was disappointed, and apart from encouraging us to work even harder to excel, she seemed to be at her wits' end.

Jing's graduation from middle school at the age of eighteen posed an immediate problem. She could either become one of the job seekers, joining an army of youngsters 'waiting for job', or she could go to a nearby village to work in the fields. My mother was nervous about the first option with its eternally long waiting list, but also had reservations about the second choice. Losing a key member of our household – Jing had effectively taken on the role of an adult since my father's death – was one thing, but there was something a lot worse. Mother's concern was not without basis, for only a short while before, I had seen Madam Guan in tears as she showed my mother a blue scarf she had bought for No. 6, her daughter who was working in a nearby village. I recall Madam Guan saying something to the effect that No. 6 could not earn enough to pay for her food and clothing even after toiling in the fields all day long.

Establishing *guanxi* was crucial in securing jobs at that time, and, unfortunately, my mother was not very good at it, as it often involved much flattering and ingratiating oneself with people who had influence. She was going to try, though, and she said that she was going to call on a Mr Chang for some help. Mr Chang was a former colleague of my father and was now a deputy head in the personnel department of the railway bureau. It was a very influential post, since the personnel department of the bureau was an extremely powerful function in our city at that time. Mr Chang had not come to visit us for many years now, in fact not since my father's death, but he was still an old contact, or so my mother tried to convince herself.

It had been some time since my mother started to talk about visiting Mr Chang. 'He will certainly be busy today, and I'll go another day,' and 'It's raining today, and I'll go tomorrow,' I heard my mother say this a few times to us, but more to herself really. She was somehow always trying to find excuses, which was rather unlike her. I remember that one day, when I came back from school, I found her smoking again. This time she didn't even try to hide it, and her eyes were filled with worries and sorrow. I never knew what happened that day, but after that she never talked about asking for help from Mr Chang again.

A few months later, in a smoky office of the personnel department in the railway bureau, Jing was waiting to see Mr Chang. She had not told our mother about her visit or indeed her plan to persuade Mr Chang to help her with a job, but both Meiling and I knew about it. We had, more than once, seen her practising her speech in front of the mirror my father had bought many years ago. Most of the time, Jing pretended she didn't notice us watching. I giggled every time she cleared her throat before delivering her speech in an upbeat and grown-up manner, but she largely managed to ignore the distraction. Occasionally, her speech would collapse in a fit of giggles which were triggered by mine. Looking back, it was a little cruel of me to giggle, and for Jing, a naturally placid and slightly shy 18-year-old, it was a big and brave thing to take on Mr Chang. She didn't have an appointment and, in any case, people didn't seem to stick to appointments anyway. She had been in that office a few times now and every time she was there, she was told either that Mr Chang was busy or he was in a meeting. Jing patiently waited until one day her patience ran out and she barged past Mr Chang's astonished assistant and straight into Mr Chang's plush office. 'Uncle Chang,' she began her well-rehearsed request, when she saw Mr Chang, a big man in his fifties, sitting close to a slender woman in her early thirties. She was very pretty, Jing told us later, and even managed to make a blue Mao suit look sexy. They were engaged in an intimate conversation. A little startled, Mr Chang opened his mouth, and then, quickly regaining his calm, took a draw at his cigarette. 'Long time no see,' he said in a friendly and avuncular voice while his lady visitor looked down in embarrassment, smoothing her hair a little.

It was not surprising that Jing's meeting with Mr Chang didn't lead to anything. 'You should go to the bastard and tell him that you are going to tell the whole world about his liaison,' Madam Guan advised my mother after she had heard about Jing's experience. 'That will soon sort him out, and sort out a job as well,' she grinned, and then added, 'That's called the art of war.' Madam Guan looked really pleased with herself for coming up with the name of a treatise written by Sun Tzu, a military strategist of the fifth century BC. She took a drag on her cigarette, then slowly blew out the smoke, and behind the smoke was a face filled with self-satisfaction. Madam Guan and her tactics did bring some much needed laughter to us, and my sister Yan even volunteered to carry out the operation. As tempting as Madam Guan's proposal was, my mother said that we must not do any such thing.

Mr Wei, another of my father's former colleagues, came to our aid. Now the Party Secretary of a large railway company, he offered to help after Madam Zhou, a colleague of my mother and a neighbour of his, had told him about our difficulties. I remember one summer evening when I went along with my mother to thank Mr Wei who had found a job for Jing in his company. The fragrance of the Chinese wisteria greeted us as we walked into their big front garden, and its lilac-blue flowers hung beautifully over the front of a neatly kept house. I was enchanted by the large rose-pink peonies and the delicate scent wafting through the garden. Madam Wei, a tall lady in her early fifties, greeted us warmly, and smiled with her big dark eyes. She seemed genuinely pleased to see us and looked fondly at me while constantly offering me snacks to eat. Mr Wei, a tall, thin man, was mild-mannered, contrary to my preconception of the stereotypical senior cadre, a word used in our city for leaders or people with senior positions. He came across as kind and considerate, and insisted that we took back a basket of eggs that Jing had bought for them as a thank-you present. Getting out a small bamboo box, Madam Wei gave me two lychees which she said had just come from the south of China. We couldn't grow lychees in our city because of the climate, and they were a real luxury to have. I still remember my excitement at seeing the fresh lychees for the first time, and their lizard-like skin fascinated me. I was thrilled by the anticipation of tasting the juicy white flesh of these beautiful fruits. One of my favourite stories at that time concerned a great beauty of the eighth century and her love for lychees. She was a favourite concubine to a Tang emperor and, in order to please her, courtiers sent men to travel some thousand miles on horseback to get fresh lychees from the south and bring them back to Xian, the then capital. No wonder, as the legend went, the favourite concubine was fragrant and smelt of roses – well, lychees, in this case.

Jing's job brought some joy back to our life. As an apprentice at a railway company near Zuozishan, a small Inner Mongolian town some forty minutes away by train, she became a breadwinner at the age of 19 and now brought home a small salary, a welcome addition to our household finances. With her first month's salary, she bought a smoked chicken, a piece of pork and some vegetables on market day in her small town. It seemed that her small town had a better food supply than our city at that time, but what was encouraging was the emergence of street markets in our city, with more small vendors selling vegetables from the backs of their carts. With the ingredients from the market, Jing set out to give us a feast.

Zuozishan smoked chicken was absolutely delicious. A delicacy in the town famous for its long history of raising succulent chicken, the flavour of the smoked chicken was enhanced by the local spring water used in the smoking and stewing of the famous chicken. To have a whole chicken was a rare luxury for us, and the legs and wings proved to be the most popular parts of it. Legs and wings were considered to be tastier than chicken breasts in China, as we thought they were better exercised and so more tender.

Jing chose a piece of streaky pork and cut it, with the skin still on, into long, thick slices. She then marinated them in a mixture of soy sauce, salt, sugar and rice wine, adding ginger, spring onions, star anise, cloves and cassia bark into the sauce. In the meantime, she toasted a small amount of glutinous rice in a wok. After a couple of hours of marinating, she coated the meat slices in the glutinous rice before arranging them carefully on a plate. She then placed the plate in a steamer and steamed for forty minutes or so, until cooked. The pork coated with glutinous rice was brilliant and packed with flavours.

Jing also cooked a simple but delicious vegetable dish. With some Chinese long leaf washed, she blanched it, drained it and then rinsed it with cold water. She neatly arranged the Chinese long leaf in a saucepan, then added chicken stock and *gouqi* berries. Leaving it on the boil for a few minutes in a pressure cooker – a new gadget she had also bought with her first month's salary – she then seasoned the vegetable with salt and finally sprinkled some finely chopped spring onions over it. It was a perfect accompaniment to an excellent meal.

One day not long after Jing had cooked the delicious meal, there was a knock on the door and a thin man in his early thirties was there, and looked hesitant when I opened the door. He appeared respectable enough, and was in an army uniform but without the usual military emblems. He asked for Yan and said that he was an army recruiting officer looking for musical talent. I looked at him, and something about him made me feel a little uneasy or even suspicious. It was not the lack of emblems as such, because I had seen, on several occasions, Auntie Song's husband wearing his army uniform without the emblems, nor was it his dirty shoes, although these were quite unsuitable for an army officer. There was something else that I could just not quite put my finger on. I asked him how he had heard about my sister, and he said that she had been referred to him by our music teacher Madam Zhang. 'That's OK, then,' I thought, and so I let him in, as the mention of Madam Zhang's name made me feel less uncomfortable.

It was a while before my mother returned, but the army recruiting officer, Mr Li, who preferred to be addressed as Comrade Li, didn't seem to mind waiting around while Meiling and I were doing our homework. As soon as I heard my mother's bicycle bell, I rushed outside to tell her about our unexpected guest. Mother was a little intrigued, to say the least, about the visit. With army opportunities being so sought after, why would a recruiting officer need to knock on the door? she wondered. Looking back, it must have been a combination of my mother's optimism and desperation that led her to give him the benefit of the doubt.

Comrade Li didn't stand up but simply nodded as she came into the house. 'Nihao,' Mother said as she made him a cup of jasmine tea, a hospitable thing to do in our city no matter what time of the day it was, and something that Meiling and I had deliberately skipped. He sounded convincing enough when he talked about his job, but started to mumble and to be very vague when answering my mother's questions. Thinking about it now, he was quite a master at steering questions in my mother's direction, and, as a result, he didn't have to disclose anything.

Comrade Li came again a couple of days later and said that he was just following up his visit, which in turn was followed up by yet another visit. With his subsequent visits, he rarely mentioned the potential recruitment but started to pry into our lives. Yan became suspicious and started to challenge him whenever she was around. We all started to smell a rat, and alarm bells rang when he suggested that he could take Meiling and me to a nearby city to audition for places in the army's university. Audition and university? His remarks startled us, and, keen to bring his visit to an end, my mother told him that there was no need for him to come again, as neither of us would be suitable to join the army. But that didn't seem to stop him, and he turned aggressive one day when Yan barred him from entering our house.

The policeman in our local police station, which mostly just dealt with residence registration, was not interested in the case when my mother reported the incident. 'Just tell him to go away,' he said to my mother. Easier said than done. My mother now decided to solicit help from our music teacher Madam

Zhang, who, after all, had apparently had dealings with Comrade Li. But Madam Zhang had never heard of Comrade Li. After our detailed description of him, she racked her brains, and finally remembered that a man of that description had briefly chatted to her at a street market when he had overheard her talking about her music students with another teacher from No. 1 Middle School.

No. 2 People's Guesthouse was located near the municipal government offices, one of the many places in our city to have names containing the word 'People's' . It was not far from the impressive-looking city museum with a sculpture of a galloping horse that Meiling and I visited often, though not as often as before she started practising martial arts at a sports school. If she could not get a job involving art, she might get into our city's martial arts school, my mother kept encouraging her to think.

One lunchtime, my mother went to the guesthouse with Madam Zhang as they wanted to talk to somebody who might help them to track down where Comrade Li actually came from. Neither the gatekeeper nor the registration lady at the guesthouse had either seen or heard of Comrade Li, who had told us that he was based there. My mother returned to the guesthouse a couple of times with Madam Zhang, but the visits didn't come to any conclusion. I am still not sure whether it was just a coincidence or whether it was as a result of these visits, but Comrade Li never showed up at our house again. Some months later, I thought I caught a glimpse of him hovering around a street market with the same uniform and the same pair of dirty shoes. I quickly turned away, because the sight of him simply made me feel uncomfortable.

Once again, my mother was talking about giving up her iron rice bowl, and this time it seemed for real. She said that some of her colleagues were beginning to retire at the age of 50 and, if she wanted to, she could do the same. 'I've only got one job and I have to give it to Yan,' she said to Meiling and me one day. She was serious about retiring so that Yan could succeed her at work. It was a new thing in our city for a parent to retire so that a son or daughter could take over the iron rice bowl. It proved popular at the time, as it got around the issue of unemployment to some degree. Yan, having recently left school, was now very unhappy with her job picking potatoes on the railway bureau's farm, and it seemed that she had given up her dream of becoming a professional musician. There was little that my mother could do to console her, particularly after Auntie Song had told her that she could not help after all.

Mother sounded really sombre when she broke the news of her imminent retirement to Meiling and me. 'I don't know what will happen to you when you finish your schooling,' she said with a deep sigh. As had happened before, neither Meiling nor I reacted to the news. Looking back now, I can see that at the age of 12 I didn't fully understand how bleak our future must have looked. There was actually no real future to talk about, and, for Meiling and me, ignorance truly was bliss.

'Look, great news.' Mother rushed excitedly in with a copy of the *People's Daily* in her hands one day several months later. She had not sounded so pleased for a long time, and she was absolutely engrossed in the headline news. 'You will be able to go to university now,' she exclaimed to Meiling and me. China was to reinstate the university entrance exams after a gap of 11 years, she read out loud. I can still remember her face and the wrinkles exaggerated by her smile. That day, my mother brought out the flute that she had not played for a very long time. Although a little rusty, she played a beautiful melody. To celebrate, she cooked cuttlefish, a favourite dish usually reserved for weekend treats. She sang as she prepared the cuttlefish under the lilac tree, on the small red wooden stool which had lost its colour somewhat over the years. The occasional splash of the ink coming out of the eyes of the cuttlefish didn't seem to bother her, and she carried on merrily. The cuttlefish was exceptional that day, because we also tasted hope.

9

Golden Phoenix and No. 1 Middle School

The river flowed to the sound of music. Not far from our house, a soprano, a plump young woman, was singing by the river. Every morning, she would start with some basic scales before singing some amazing pieces, which my mother told me were from western operas. I loved her beautiful long dark hair; she looked so elegant with it hanging loose to below her shoulders. It was quite daring to wear long hair like that in our city, quite different from the plaits, pigtails or plain short hair that we had been used to, and it was certainly a new trend that I had started to notice lately. Previously, flaunting long hair loose like that would have been considered decadent and would most probably have been publicly criticised. 'You should eat plenty of sesame,' our neighbour Madam Jiao advised me authoritatively when I said that I envied the long dark hair.

I saw the lady every morning on the riverbank where I went to practise my English by speaking out loud. I loved the fresh air and the open space, and besides I did not feel so embarrassed at my far from perfect pronunciation, because my audience, a herd of Mr Ma's Friesian cows, were far from critical. Grazing happily on the meadows, they would occasionally look up and stare at me, with a slight look of bewilderment. I carried on nevertheless.

Singing western songs and speaking English publicly were new things at that time, which we could not have done, or would not have dared to do, before. I had started learning English some years earlier during a visit from my uncle who lived in Tianjin, a city near Beijing. I remember him spending quite some time tuning our Panda radio, with his tall, thin body leaning against our walnut desk, occasionally looking a little puzzled. Madam Guan often complimented my uncle on his 'western' nose, which embarrassed him a little. She used to say that his nose, bigger and higher bridged compared to the smaller and flatter noses of most Chinese, reminded her of a handsome European she had seen in Tianjin where she had lived briefly as a young girl in the 1930s. 'The French knew how to build nice houses, and my word, those amazing wooden staircases,' Madam Guan used to exclaim when entertaining us with the story of her visiting, as a young girl, one of those large houses in the French Concession. 'Mind you, the squeaking floorboards would drive me mad now,' she often added, with a nostalgic smile, between taking yet another deep drag on her cigarette. I didn't have much idea about what Madam Guan was talking about at that time, except that I faintly understood that under some unfair treaties, certain territories in Tianjin, a port city, had been ceded by the Qing government to the French and British around the turn of the century. As to my uncle's nose, since I had never seen a westerner in real life, I could not really relate to what she said about it at all. Meiling and I used to joke that Madam Guan was only saying this because she wanted to chat to my uncle about Tianjin, her dear home town, as she often called it.

It seemed difficult for my uncle to get the frequency he wanted on the radio, and, when he did, the reception was often accompanied by hissing and crackling noises. An extension to the aerial did the trick and then, I recall, came a beautiful voice reading an equally beautiful-sounding piece. 'Leaves of Grass', my uncle, who was an economist fluent in both Japanese and English, repeated the words to me. I didn't understand any of it but the sound of the words fascinated me. My uncle, who helped us financially every month, was encouraged by my interest and he set out to teach me some English straight away. With the help of the aerial extension, our Panda radio did well, and continued to bring us Voice of America. I soon became hooked on it, and VOA became my teacher after my uncle returned home, but I had to keep it quiet, my mother told me, in case somebody reported us to the authorities for being pro-imperialist, a serious accusation. I recall the hot summer days when we had to keep the windows and door firmly closed in order to listen to VOA. It was all pretty secretive, and one day I nearly broke our reliable Panda when some members of the residential committee of our neighbourhood came to our house unexpectedly. 'Why do they keep all the windows shut,' one loud-voiced woman in her late forties said, disapprovingly, as she knocked on our door one warm Sunday morning. I had been totally immersed in my listening, but the knock brought me rudely back to reality. I quickly reached out for the off switch and in doing so nearly knocked the radio off the round table it was on.

They were here to check on the hygiene and cleanliness of our house – it was quite common at that time for the residential committee to call at each household, sometimes with a little notice and sometimes without. 'It is patriotic to clean and to contribute to good public health,' Madam Wang, the leader of the committee, repeated this mantra whenever she came around, almost to warn off any potential protest about their visits. It didn't always work. She criticised us during one of her visits when she spotted a pane of broken glass in our window. With its two broken parts being held together, perhaps a little precariously, by strips of newspaper glued to them, it is fair to say that it was not the prettiest picture. 'How can a house of girls tolerate such shabbiness!' Madam Wang said loudly, pointing at the yellowing newspaper, and her short hair moved vigorously as she shook her head with an air of helplessness and disapproval. 'Yes, quite,' Yan, the most excitable of us four girls, got into one of her combative moods. 'How can a leader like you not arrange for the repair man to come and repair it after we have reported it not once, not twice, but three times?' she lashed out, mimicking Madam Wang's tone, to the giggles of Meiling and me and the loud cheers from Guan No. 8, who seemed to have a knack for being present on such occasions. Spurred on by her audience, Yan was in her element. 'Oh, I see, because they are busy painting your windows,' she added in a truly masterful act of mimicry, and obviously without the intention of sparing any feelings. Madam Wang seemed to lose her usual calm and eloquence for once. 'That's nonsense,' she mumbled, before quickly summoning her team, most of whom were now trying hard to suppress their amusement, to move on to check on another family. It is perhaps worth mentioning that people in our neighbourhood, like most people in China, didn't own their homes at that time. We and all our neighbours were tenants of the railway bureau, who, as landlord, provided maintenance through its own maintenance companies. As always, there was a queue for things to be done and in our case, painting the leader's windows was clearly being given priority over mending our broken glass. Suffice to say, Yan's act had some impact and as it happened, our pane of glass was repaired soon after the episode.

Now I no longer needed to listen to VOA in secret, and, just like the soprano, I relished this newfound freedom. There had definitely been a change of atmosphere in our neighbourhood since Mao's death and the subsequent downfall of the Gang of

Four with Mao's wife as the ringleader. I still remember the joy and jubilation felt among people that day in 1976 when our city celebrated the end of the ten-year-long Cultural Revolution. I noticed that adults started to talk more openly, without looking around, and people began to behave in a more relaxed way to each other. The constant fear of being reported and reprimanded by the Red Guards and revolutionary activists, who now kept a very low profile, seemed to be ebbing away. It felt as though a dark cloud had been lifted from above us, and our neighbour-hood was filled with more laughter and fun.

That summer brought an end to my primary school days. It also filled me with some considerable satisfaction and pride that I had completed my reading of the Stories of Lei Feng, a thick book filled with many stories about Comrade Lei Feng, a model soldier whom Chairman Mao had called upon the nation to learn from. For many months I had religiously read the accounts of the many selfless acts of the young model soldier. I read them to the whole school from the small desk in the broadcasting room during the morning exercise time. I can almost still feel the blush in my face when the head of education department from the railway bureau praised my reading during her official visit to our school, but I was truly pleased. Although sad to leave my broadcasting room, I was really looking forward to joining Meiling at No. I Middle School. No. I Middle School was affili-ated to the railway bureau which at the time had four primary schools and four middle schools. It was quite common at that time for a big employer such as the railway bureau to have its own schools and hospitals. With a long summer holiday after the exams, I took it upon myself to do the food shopping for our family, primarily buying vegetables. We used to buy vegeta-bles fresh every day, as we loved fresh produce and in any case lacked storage space. Lately, more street markets had started to emerge and small vendors, mostly farmers from the suburbs, began to appear. The farmers were the true vanguard of the market economy. They took advantage of the growing demand and supplied the city people with fresh fruits and vegetables, which they loaded on their donkey carts or transported in baskets tied to the backs of their bicycles, normally at a higher price than we would pay at the state-owned shops. The small vendors were extremely popular, as they provided more choice and fresher produce. I still remember the day when my mother bought a cut of pork from a farmer in the street market. It was the first time in my memory that we were able to buy a piece of decent pork without any vouchers. 'From my favourite pig,' the farmer said of the beautiful meat he proudly displayed in a glass cabinet. 'And the pig has got a name as well,' he told us. I smiled and was just amazed at his openness, a million miles from the clandestine egg swapping not so long ago, with the eggs hidden in the farmers' canvas tool-bags. 'One *yuan* and thirty-seven *fen* in change,' I volunteered almost as soon as the farmer had finished weighing the pork on his simple scale. 'Sure?' he teased me after a pause, and I nodded, confident of my mental arithmetic. He smiled. 'I bet you will be the golden phoenix of your neighbourhood one day,' he joked. Golden phoenix was a term we used in our city at that time to refer to somebody with the ability to excel in his or her environment.

There were still queues at the state-owned shops, and they were still quite long, but nothing like as long as they used to be in the days when my sister Yan used to get up early to join them at the crack of dawn. I had devised quite a clever method of speeding things up. I would join the queue as normal, usually on the way back from school, then, after staying in the queue for ten minutes or so, I would tell somebody either just in front of me or just behind me that I needed to fetch some money and ask them to keep my place for me. Then I would run home and fetch some change from an old Chinese medicine box, now used as our money box. By the time I returned to my place in the queue, it would often have moved near the front of the queue. Like this, I made good use of my time and cut quite a lot of time out of queuing. Of course, my method didn't always work. Sometimes, neither the person in front nor behind wanted to help hold my place, and sometimes, even though one or even two people offered to help, I had to join the queue again because I was just that bit too late, and missed my place.

One day I cooked some delicious meatballs all on my own. I gathered together a large piece of ginger, a couple of spring onions and a few cloves of garlic, and started the preparation. With a big chopping knife, I bashed the garlic with the back of the blade in the same way as I had seen my mother doing. By doing so, the skin should come off easily, although not so easily for me on the first attempt. It worked the second time, though, when I bashed the garlic harder. Chopping the garlic, spring onions and ginger finely was not as easy as it sounded either, and everything seemed to conspire against me. I tried to be patient and kept on chopping, but it didn't even sound right. Instead of sounding like a professional orchestra playing, my chopping sounded like an amateur struggling with an out-of-tune instrument. I persisted nevertheless, until finally I got the end result I was happy with. Adding the finely chopped ginger, garlic and spring onions to the minced pork, I stirred and mixed everything together in a mixing bowl. I then added a little corn-flour, some soy sauce, a pinch of herbs and a splash of sesame oil before I seasoned the mix with salt and pepper. Just to be a little different, I also added a green pepper, finely chopped. With all the ingredients prepared, I scooped the mixture into pieces and then rolled each piece into a small round ball before I put them neatly on to a plate, ready to be steamed.

While the meatballs happily steamed, I set out to cook bean curd fried with Chinese long leaf. Giving the whole block of fresh bean curd a quick rinse, I cut it into strips and then cut the Chinese long leaf into similar pieces. I poured some oil into the wok and then added a few Chinese peppercorns to get a little spiciness into the oil. I waited for the oil to get really hot before I added the slices of bean curd and then left them until both sides were golden brown. I then added a few pieces of roughly chopped spring onion and all the Chinese long leaf. A good stir and, a few minutes later, with a final bit of seasoning, the dish was done.

The meatballs went down really well with the fried bean curd and Chinese long leaf, accompanied by boiled rice. We usually had rice and millet, which was cheaper, boiled together, but I decided to push the boat out and leave out the millet, considering I had just bought some rice from a farmer who had sold it to me from a flaxen sack attached to his bicycle. A little surprised by the impromptu cooking, my first solo attempt, everybody in the family seemed to genuinely enjoy the food. Even Madam Guan looked impressed when she saw what I had cooked. 'Not bad for a 12-year-old,' she said with a nod of approval. Coming from a critical cook like her, that was a high accolade indeed. I walked around really pleased with myself for quite a few days afterwards.

Back at school, the old school gatekeeper didn't smile at me. He continued smoking his pipe, behind which he always used to smile every morning when he handed me the key to the broadcasting room. A little surprised, I said that I had come for the results of my finals and for the acceptance notice from No. 1 Middle School. Now removing the pipe from his mouth a little, he cleared his throat before he gestured with his head in the direction of two piles of paper on an old desk. The two piles both looked a little untidy, with the one on the left being a bit smaller than the other. I started with the smaller pile and was eagerly looking for the sheet of paper with my results and acceptance notice on. The papers didn't seem to be in any particular order and so I ploughed on with the same patience of a passenger whose luggage is always the last to turn up. There were about two hundred pupils in my year at my school, so I was prepared for it to take a while.

The old man mumbled something and then continued smoking his pipe. I glanced at him and he looked subdued. 'The other pile,' he said finally, and his words were followed by a cough. He was right, and towards the top of the second pile, I found the piece of paper with my name on. My heart jumped and beat fast as I looked quickly at the results column and then the middle school acceptance notice. I simply could not believe my eyes.

It was not that I didn't do well with my finals, quite the contrary, I did exceptionally well in all subjects except PE. Even my PE result was adequate – though, to be truthful, I was sure Teacher Liu had rewarded me with some extra marks for my willingness to try. Yet, in spite of my good exam results, I had not been accepted by No. 1 Middle School, the school I had so looked forward to. Instead, I had to stay on at my current school for another year because No. 1 didn't have the capacity to cope with the volume of school leavers in my year. 'It's the same, the two schools,' the gatekeeper said with a sigh. 'It's not the same,' I replied, trying to fight back the tears. I now know why he didn't smile at me that day, because he knew I would be heartbroken.

The cheers from the pupils celebrating their entrance to No. 1 Middle School got louder, and I looked on with envy. 'We might be in the same class,' my friend Hong said enthusiastically. Like me, she had taken it for granted that I would automatically go to No. 1, as our neighbourhood was in its catchment area and all my sisters went there. As the first middle school established under the railway bureau in our city some years ago, the school boasted a pleasant atmosphere and retained some truly brilliant teachers. Hong's remark made it impossible for me to hold back the tears any longer. I so wished I could be part of the cheering crowd.

It didn't take me long to find out that most of the pupils who were chosen for No. 1 Middle School happened to have parents working in the railway bureau itself or the affiliated hospital, universally recognised as an important and influential place to work. 'If only your father were alive,' my mother said with a sigh when I told her about this. 'You will do well wherever you are,' she said, resuming her usual optimism. 'It is closer, and you might have good teachers anyway,' she added, trying to comfort me. I was now old enough to know that my mother hated to ask for favours, so I figured that I had to do it myself if I wanted a change in my luck. My first call was on Teacher Liu. As soon as he saw me, he knew what it was all about. 'Our school will be just as good,' Teacher Liu said, with his hand touching his nose; he obviously felt uneasy. 'Besides, you could continue with your broadcasting,' he said, trying to help me see the bright side. It was not the same, I argued, and if it were the same, why were the pupils with good connections all going to No. 1?' 'It all comes down to the old *guanxi* again,' I complained to Teacher Liu tearfully. To be fair to him, he was very disappointed for me as well. He did try to talk to the headmaster who insisted that he could not remove anybody from No. 1's list just to fit me in. My first attempt had failed.

I joined a small group of five girls and two boys. Every morning, we turned up outside the headmaster's office at our school, moments after he arrived for work. We then stood in front of his window until he paid attention to us, and then started to demand that he added us to the No. 1's list. The headmaster, a stocky man probably in his late forties, tried his best to ignore us and occasionally he would say, quite calmly, that we were wasting our time and his. Every day, we stayed as long as he did in school, and soon learnt to ignore him when he told us off. His patience, although pretty impressive, was finally worn out after a week or so of persistent badgering by seven teenagers, and one day he reacted. Gathering us together, he told us severely that we lacked respect and good behaviour, and in fact we were a nuisance. His criticism didn't upset me as much as it might; somehow it excited me a little, as I saw his anger as a sort of prelude to some action. We, our group, looked at each other, somewhat knowingly but nervously. It felt as if our fate would be sealed there and then.

The truth was that the headmaster, totally fed up with us, signed each of us off on a piece of headed notepaper saying that we were no longer with his school. In theory, we could now take our dossier, this piece of paper and our exam results, to any middle school which might take us. 'You are on your own if you cannot get a place,' he said as he signed my paper, but I was too excited to take his warning seriously. I waved goodbye to my primary school of five years, with the headmaster's signature on the school's official notepaper.

I got on to my mother's Russian bicycle, but the years had taken some of the elegance off this once stylish lady's bike. No. 1 Middle School was some fifteen minutes away by bike, and I could not get there soon enough. The large playground was filled with chirping and laughing and some boys were chasing each other around for fun. It was morning exercise time and the loudspeaker was playing some pre-exercise music. It was a perfect early autumn day, clear and bright. I parked my bicycle and headed to the staff rooms. I took a deep breath before I knocked on the door of the biology department.

Madam Wu was surprised to see me. She had not seen me for a while, in fact not since I stopped taking violin lessons from her son Jiang. To be honest, I was quite embarrassed to see Madam Wu, because I had given up my violin lessons for no obvious reason. Jiang had been a really good teacher and he had always willingly given his time to me, even though teaching me had often taken up quite a big chunk of his holiday time. I had persisted with learning and practising for some time, but it had been quite hard to have a teacher who was mostly away in the army. My sister Yan's unsuccessful pursuit of a professional musical career did nothing to encourage me to continue. In short, I had given up my violin. Looking back, I still feel a little bad about letting down Madam Wu, Jiang and my uncle who had saved to buy the violin for me. But if there is any consolation, the early introduction to the violin has given me a love for music which I don't think will ever diminish.

Madam Wu was all smiles when she saw the results of my exams. 'Very well done,' she said. To my relief, she didn't mention my violin lessons. After having a quick chat with a colleague, she asked me to follow her to the sports ground. By now, the sports ground was more orderly, with all the pupils doing a set of morning exercises to the radio music. Madam Wu chatted to Teacher Zhang, a slender and sporty-looking woman in her late twenties, before showing her my dossier. 'Younger sister of Yan, no problem,' she said with a smile behind her big round eyes; she had obviously previously taught my sister Yan.

'Go and join in the exercises,' Teacher Zhang said to me. I didn't move, because I could not believe my ears. 'Don't just stand there,' she said in her direct style. I ran to join her class in the middle of exercises, my heart jumping with excitement. And so it was that I became a proud pupil of Teacher Zhang's class at No. 1 Middle School.

'What are you doing here?' Meiling ran to catch me after the pupils all dispersed after the exercises. Being at the front with Madam Wu and Teacher Zhang had made me stand out. Meiling was absolutely amazed at my triumph, and so was my friend Hong, who came to me with her mouth wide open. 'Well I never,' she said. But the person who was the most surprised was perhaps me, because that very morning I had nearly given up hope of studying at No. 1.

I was the lucky one in our group of seven, the only one to get into No. 1 Middle School. After some failed attempts, four of the group reluctantly went to No. 2 and the others went to No. 3, both of which were second-rate compared to No. 1. I could not wait to tell my mother about my news, and she was truly delighted when she saw my happy face later that day when I came back from No. 1 Middle School.

10

University Dream

The low bridge across the river near No. 1 Middle School often became very congested at lunchtime. With an army of bicycles joining from our school, with over a thousand pupils in five forms, it was hardly surprising. Most pupils lived in our neighbourhood or in the adjacent ones, and a lot of us chose to ride to school. Bicycle riding could not get tougher with a flood of bicycles coming out of the school gate all at the same time, with hungry youngsters eager to get home as early as possible. There was a small canteen in our school, but it only catered for a small group of boarders whose parents mostly worked in the railway companies and were based in small towns too far away for them to commute. Some of the boarders attended our school because there were no middle schools in their towns, while others attended because of its good reputation and the higher level of teaching, so I was told. With the after-school congestion, it was often very hard to have enough space even to mount the bike. Sometimes, we had to compete for road space with people finishing work at the same time. To make things worse, horse carts and mule carts usually joined the busy traffic as well, accompanied by some big 'iron oxen', of which we saw a lot more now in our city since I had first heard about them from cousin Shengli a few years before. The tractors were very noisy, and the fumes from them were quite awful, especially if you happened to be stuck behind one on your bicycle. In the long cold winter, the air was particularly unpleasant, with fumes, dust and coal smoke pouring out of thousands of low chimneys from the city's dwellings and boiler houses. I remember the yellow sky we had in winter, and often the white mouth masks we used to wear to protect us from the extreme cold and from the fumes were absolutely covered in black dust. The only oasis near us seemed to be a cemetery for *Huis*, the Chinese Muslims, which was surrounded by evergreen trees. There were apricot trees inside as well, Lanlan, our neighbour Mr Ma's daughter, had told me, and the cemetery faced Mecca, she added mysteriously. I didn't really understand then what Mecca was and its significance. I simply nodded when she told me about it all.

Lately, I had also noticed that the river near us had started to dry up a little, and even the once beautiful meadows on the riverbank started to lose their lushness. My mother said this was because of the drought we had been experiencing. In Huhehot, we didn't have a lot of rain, but sometimes we had artificial rain. I was quite fascinated when my mother explained that under certain weather conditions, rain could be induced through some chemical reaction triggered by a piece of artillery firing chemicals into the sky above the city. Mother always seemed to take a keen interest in what was going on in our environment, but sometimes this could result in some quite embarrassing situations.

Recently there had started to be an unpleasant odour coming from the river. Mother said one day after a long walk along the river that she thought she had traced the cause of the problem. She then set out to write a long letter to a pharmaceutical company nearby which she believed was discharging its waste water into the river without proper treatment. I remember she read through her rather long letter several times before she put it into an envelope. A month passed without her getting a reply, and so she sent the letter again, but still there was no reply. So she went to the company's site and demanded to see the

Communist Party Secretary, the most senior person there. There were party secretaries at all levels, even at the level of the residential committee of our neighbourhood. Madam Jiao, our neighbour, used to talk about the Party Secretary of the railway bureau, or the Supreme as she referred to him, with some considerable awe, almost as if she were star-struck. When my mother arrived, 'He is busy,' the gatekeeper, a thin man in his fifties, said expressionlessly and barred her from going through the factory gate. My mother then went to the grain store in our neighbourhood to borrow their phone, as we didn't have our own phone then. The operator at the pharmaceutical company was equally unhelpful. 'He will reply in due course,' she said before slamming the phone down.

Mother didn't give up easily and she then went to raise the issue with the residential committee of our neighbourhood. She was quite hopeful that the committee would be receptive to her complaint and would do something about it. If nothing else, it would at least do something for the benefit of the residents it represented, my mother thought. She was quite encouraged when Madam Wang, the leader of the committee, agreed to listen to her. After my mother had voiced her complaint, there was a long pause before the leader started to speak. 'You should be more understanding to the company, and to the people who contribute to our socialist economy,' said Madam Wang, who had a habit of quoting things from the papers. She then cleared her throat a little, and added that as an old and educated comrade, my mother perhaps should use her energy on something more useful. 'Maybe she has a really long memory and is just trying to get her own back,' Meiling tried to console my mother by reminding her of when Yan had challenged Madam Wang about our broken window. Meiling's remark put a little smile back on to the face of my mother, who was clearly very disappointed with the outcome of the meeting. All in all, my mother's action plan had failed. That didn't seem to stop her from voicing her concern about this sort of thing, about which she felt quite passionately. Once, she became very incensed, quite unlike her, when Guan No. 4 said excitedly that his employer, a leather company, was going to cut down some trees to create more storage space. 'We are only trying to make a living,' he said, implying that my mother was not living in the real world. 'But that doesn't mean we should destroy our environment,' she insisted. It was quite an unhappy interaction, with both No. 4 and my mother feeling totally misunderstood. No. 4 did have a point, though, and at that time people's main focus was on producing more food and more of everything that we had been deprived of for so long, regardless of the damage to our environment. My mother was perhaps just a little too much ahead of her time.

'Read after me,' I stood at the podium in our classroom and addressed a class of forty. It was the morning revision time before the main classes started at eight. With the authority given to me by Teacher Zhang, even the most mischievous pupil had to behave himself when I was 'teaching' them English. Teacher Zhang wanted her class to excel in all subjects. An inspiring maths teacher herself, she made algebra really interesting, and $x+y$ became more than just mathematical symbols. To whet my appetite and that of a couple of boys, Teacher Zhang used to give us extra problems to solve every day. I took to this like a duck to water and absolutely loved every bit of it. I was a model pupil and the little pet of Teacher Zhang, who indulged me in everything, well, nearly everything.

The parents' meetings often took place after exams, which

we usually had at the beginning, in the middle and at the end of each of the two terms in the school year. After each exam, Teacher Zhang would 'publish' league tables showing how pupils had performed in major subjects like maths, Chinese language, English and, later, physics and chemistry. The league tables were always well presented on a large sheet of red paper with the results written in beautiful Chinese calligraphy, and they were often the focus of the parents' meetings, which mostly took place in the evenings or at weekends. This was all pretty incredible, because only a few years previously, very few parents were remotely interested in the results. 'Better to have an influential father than to do well in sciences,' was the popular saying in our city, and one that I absolutely detested.

'My mother cannot come because she is on the evening shift,' I said to Teacher Zhang one day before another imminent meeting, a mantra I had used quite a few times. I have to say I didn't enjoy doing this, and that was probably why on the previous occasion, I had handed her a slip with my mother's apologies written on the back of a sheet of desk calendar. It seemed to work pretty well, and Teacher Zhang said nothing, just nodding in acknowledgement. But this time, instead of giving her usual acknowledgement, Teacher Zhang looked a little pensive. 'When is your mother going to be free to come?' she asked after a pause. 'All the parents have been saying that they want to get some advice from your mother, to see how you have managed to be near the top of every league table,' she added, looking straight into my eyes. 'She has no advice to give,' I mumbled, for the first time trying to avoid her big eyes; I was truly embarrassed and a little ashamed.

My mother was in fact free to attend nearly all the parents' meetings, but most of the time she didn't know about them, because I didn't tell her. When she did ask about them, I tried my hardest to steer her away from attending, saying that it was unnecessary for every parent to attend. I can still feel my uneasiness at producing those slips with her apologies, allegedly written by my mother but in fact scribbled by me. Thinking about it now, it was impossible for Teacher Zhang not to have recognised my handwriting. To her credit, she never said a word about them.

The truth was that I was a little embarrassed by my mother, not herself as a person but her clothes. Apart from the blue railway uniform, my mother hardly had any new clothes, nothing decent anyway. Since my father's death, her salary was hardly enough to sustain us day by day, and we had only managed with my uncle's help. Although things were getting better with Jing now working, my mother's priority was always to give us more, often at the cost of sacrificing her own needs. There started to be more choices in our city now, not only with food, but also with clothes, and my mother was keen to buy us each something whenever she could. Looking back, I can still feel the guilt I felt for telling the white lies and for being embarrassed by my mother. But my guilt was often reduced a little by my own justification that I was also genuinely protecting my mother. So many ambitious parents talked endlessly at those meetings about what great things they did to encourage their children to do well in school. It was almost like a competition between parents who had great expectations for their children to shine, or to become dragons as we described it. The path to becoming a dragon, it seemed at that time, was to get a much-coveted university place. One regular 'competition' item at the parents meetings appeared to be about superfoods for memory and concentration. I remember that a drink called *mairujing*, an extract of malt and milk, was highly tipped as the popular new brain food if taken daily, but it was expensive and there was no way that my mother could afford to give us that every day. There was, however, one drink we had regularly then, and it was made from nothing other than starch that we had extracted from our own potatoes. With this drink, we would mix a large spoonful of starch, a generous amount of sugar and some cold water into a thin paste, and then add boiling water gradually while constantly beating until it achieved a consistency of whipping cream. To be honest, the drink, best drunk when hot, was not particularly great, but it introduced a little variation.

By this time, the food supply in our city was improving in both quantity and quality. We now had more supplies, thanks, largely, to the emergence of street markets and farmers selling freely, which also brought about more choices for us. It seemed that the ration vouchers were slowly losing their worth. My mother's love for seafood was much satisfied when the shop that used to provide us with the occasional cuttlefish started to stock more fish, both more varieties and more regularly. One day my mother came back, quite pleased with her purchase of a few hairtail, or ribbon fish as they were known in our city. As she took the fish from the newspaper they were wrapped in, I thought how strange-looking these silvery fish were, with their compressed white bodies tapering into a thin tail.

Heating oil in the wok, my mother added finely chopped ginger, garlic and spring onions, a spoonful of hot chilli sauce, and stirred until a distinct fragrance emerged. She then added water, a little sugar, rice wine and salt before putting in the fish, cleaned and prepared beforehand. She then brought it to the boil and then left it to simmer on medium heat until the fish was cooked. The ribbon fish, in spite of my initial reservations about its appearance, tasted delicious. Accompanied by steamed white-flour buns, it was a perfect meal. With rice now becoming more widely available, my mother liked to finish the meal with rice congee, or porridge as we called it. After this, she would sometimes buy salted ribbon fish, now available all year around. She would clean and prepare them before cutting each fish into several chunks, which she would then dip into a thin batter before frying them in a wok with a generous amount of heated oil. This often made a good and quick meal, with fried Chinese long-leaf in vinegar and sugar sauce. For this Chinese long-leaf dish, mother didn't use the leaf but only the stalk. After slicing it into big diamond-shaped pieces, she lightly fried it in heated oil. Transferring it on to a plate from the wok, she then added some boiled water and soy sauce to the wok and brought it to the boil, before adding a generous amount of sugar and a thin cornflour paste. Mixing it all thoroughly, she then transferred the lightly fried Chinese leaf back to the wok. A quick stir later, and it was ready to serve. The Chinese leaf tasted tender and fresh, and the vinegar added a really good finish to the flavour. Mother liked to cook this dish, and had by now more or less perfected it with the help of a colleague who proudly told her that she had learnt how to cook it in Zhejiang. 'The place of its origin,' she insisted.

The league tables had started to become more significant in our school lately. Now, apart from being published at the parents' meetings, the latest tables were soon to be used as a means of rearranging the classes, as Teacher Zhang announced one day. The top fifteen from each of the five classes in our year would be brought together into two 'key' classes, while the rest would be reorganised into three other classes. This reorganisation was a new thing in our school, and part of the new trend in our city at that time. Looking back, it was almost unthinkable that this could have happened just a few years previously, and the key classes and the league tables would definitely have been condemned as elitist. The reorganisation was a really major development in our school, and getting into a key class was seen as a milestone in the path of realising the dream of going to university, which our whole city seemed to harbour now, thanks to the nationwide re-introduction of the university entrance exam.

After Teacher Zhang's 'chat' with me about my mother's absence at parents' meetings, I no longer felt able not to tell my mother about them any more. In any case, my mother was very happy to attend them. On the day of the parents' meeting that had been arranged to coincide with the reorganisation of the classes, she put on one of her newest pieces of clothing, a blue cotton jacket, freshly washed and ironed. She smiled at me when I watched her combing her prematurely greying hair in front of a mirror before she set off. The mandarin collar of her jacket framed her thin but beautiful face, and her smile made me feel sad and a little ashamed of my ploy of stopping her from attending the previous meetings. 'You will be in the first key class,' my mother said to me when she returned from the meeting, and her big almond eyes were filled with joy. It was not my mother's style to clasp her hands and praise us loudly, and I didn't mind it that much, because I knew, from her eyes, that she was really pleased for me. 'You did it even without me buying the *mairujing*,' she said with some guilt. 'I don't even like the stuff that much,' I said of the drink, which I had had twice, and had actually enjoyed both times, but I wanted to make her feel better.

I was really pleased that Teacher Zhang was in charge of the first key class, which was considered to be superior even to the other key class in my year. In the few first weeks following the reorganisation, I recall, Teacher Zhang had had quite a few parents visiting her and asking for favours. In most cases, she told the parents that there was no room for any extra pupils in her prestigious class. 'She just has to work harder next time,' I once heard her saying, in her direct style, to a displeased and disappointed mother. In a few cases, though, even Teacher Zhang had to bow to the pressure from the headmaster to create a few places for pupils who happened to have extremely good connections.

Teacher Zhang's restructured class was a fun and stimulating place to be. Teacher Zhang was quite liberal and would often encourage debate or even tolerate disagreement with her at times, which could not be said about all the teachers. There was friendly rivalry in the class, and much bantering after class. 'Say that again?' teased a mischievous Zhu Liping, exaggeratedly cradling his large ears in his hands. 'What do you mean, it only took you five minutes?' he continued as I boasted to my friend Hong, also in the first key class, how I had solved a difficult algebra question really quickly. 'Don't tell me it only took you one minute, or perhaps zero minutes, to work that out, maths genius,' I answered back. 'I thought he was called Big Ears, not maths genius,' Hong joined in. 'Big Ears' was a nickname Zhu Liping had inherited from our days at primary school. 'Don't be so negative about large ears. It's very lucky to have them,' he said cheerfully, rolling his eyes cheekily behind his glasses, with their lenses as thick as the bottom of a beer bottle.

Cheerful was what I was trying to be in one of our weekly art classes when Teacher Fu gave her critique of my drawing of an enamelled mug that she had casually, or perhaps artistically in her view, put on the podium. 'Look at that, you could almost count them,' she held up my sketchbook and exclaimed in her thick local accent, which often made her sound comical. 'They are like hairs, and you can count them,' she added sarcastically, pointing to the background I had just done. As if that were not enough, she started counting the 'hairs' to the laughter of my classmates and to my own embarrassment. 'Next time, at least try to get a few tips from your sister,' she shook her head disapprovingly. I just wanted to hide, and felt humiliated by her criticism, which seemed totally unfair. It was perhaps true that I should have finished the background more finely and carefully instead of doing it coarsely and unevenly with strokes resembling 'hairs', in Teacher Fu's words; but my drawing was by no means bad by average standards. I thought of protesting, but soon thought better of it. Teacher Fu was not somebody to argue with and, in fact, I would go as far as to say that it was very risky for your life at school to even think about debating with her. She could come across as being very defensive, and I recall one incident when a girl named Hua insisted on using coloured chalks instead of the pencils that we had been asked to use. Not that she was being particularly difficult, Hua was simply very proud of her new possessions. Instead of letting her use the chalks, Teacher Fu lashed out at her, and it seemed that she saw Hua's insistence on using chalks as a challenge and threat to her authority which she fiercely protected at all times. 'Pride comes before a fall, you know,' Teacher Fu presented our class with the saying as she walked out of classroom, with a self-satisfied smirk, when break came. 'Just very jealous,' Zhu Liping murmured to me from across the aisle where he sat. As soon as Teacher Fu was out of the door, he rolled his eyes cheekily, something he did often, and then mimicked her, in the most vivid manner. That certainly cheered me up and amused everybody in our class.

The episode with Teacher Fu soon became something of the distant past the minute I saw my mother and the exceptional pyramid-like parcels she was making. *Zongzi* were delicious to eat. It was the Dragon Boat Festival, which falls on the fifth day of the fifth month in the Chinese lunar calendar, normally somewhere in June. As with most Chinese festivals, we have special food to celebrate this traditional festival and *zongzi* have been an unmissable treat for centuries. Choosing a piece of fresh bamboo leaf, washed and soaked in cold water, Mother carefully and skilfully folded one large part of the leaf into a triangle-shaped parcel. Then, she would add the filling of glutinous rice and a couple of dates, or a portion of sweetened bean paste, before sealing the parcel with the remaining part of the leaf. Finally, she would tie the parcel with a piece of string Yan had cut out from reed leaves before putting the finished product in a bowl of cold water, until it was time to steam. 'You're a lucky person,' our neighbour, Madam Guan exclaimed. As usual, she could not resist coming over and giving my mother a few festival tips, puffing on her cigarette the whole time. She was commenting on our fresh bamboo leaves, considered superior to the reed leaves which were normally used in our city and in other parts of the north where bamboo did not grow easily because of the climate. 'Smell the fragrance,' she picked up one leaf and inhaled, to the amusement of Meiling and me, who could not help but giggle. 'Aunt Guan, they don't believe you can actually smell anything because of your cigarette,' Yan was not one to keep quiet and she teased Madam Guan while helping my mother make *zongzi*. But Madam Guan was too preoccupied with the bamboo leaves, and, apart from giving Meiling and me a 'what do you know' look, she took little notice of our cheekiness. She looked genuinely impressed when my mother told her that Zhu Liping's parents had given us the leaves, from the package sent over to them by their friends in the south, where fresh bamboo leaves were the ultimate ingredients to use for making divine *zongzi*.

The Dragon Boat Festival was not all about *zongzi*, and in our city we sometimes also had a 'dry' dragon boat race – a boat race on land – as part of the celebration. I remember the first time that I saw a group of people dancing in the street and imitating the movement of rowing behind a dragon head, shaped as if it were on the prow of a boat. Mother explained to me that they were simulating the dragon boat race that people in the south had on their rivers and lakes. Guan Jie – Guan No. 8 – would never miss out on any festival fun, and not long after Madam Guan's appreciation of our bamboo leaves he came into our house with the Chinese character *wang*, which means the king, proudly painted on to his forehead using thick yellow rice wine. 'It will chase away evil,' he said, making a face at me as if he were a fierce tiger, while pointing out, exaggeratedly, every single stroke of the character on his forehead. According to Madam Guan, the character, with the strokes resembling the stripes on a tiger's forehead, would chase away evil and poison, with the help of the medicinal qualities of the yellow rice wine. Madam Guan was very superstitious and a great believer in such things, and even I resisted the temptation to giggle this time.

I loved the records my uncle sent, along with the record player he bought from a second-hand shop in Tianjin where he lived. It took a long time for my mother to persuade him to stop sending us money every month, now that we had two salaries again, with Jing working. In spite of his promise to stop, he still sent us money, but more in the form of books, records and, in this case, the record player. I remember my excitement at seeing the amazing yellow leather box, and seeing the arm and turntable inside the box at work for the first time Thinking about it now, I can almost still hear a beautiful violin concerto played on one of the records. The concerto was *Liangzhu*, or *The Butterfly Lovers*, which was named after the old Chinese love story that the music was inspired by. Often compared to the story of Romeo and Juliet, it told of two young lovers, Liang and Zhu, who could, sadly, only be united in death. I remember that my mother was totally immersed in this lyrical, moving piece which depicts the two lovers soaring happily together, at the end, as two beautiful butterflies.

The arrival of the Linguaphone course, among other records, was a timely and much-welcomed addition to my English learning. My uncle, aware of my progress in English, thought that a Linguaphone course would be a good idea for me to use to teach myself. Having now rather grown out of Voice of America, I was eager to learn more, particularly after Teacher Zhang had put me in charge of the morning class revision which involved reading aloud and grammar revision. Lately, one thing had started to bother me somewhat, and I began to feel a little frustrated when some of my grammar-related questions could not be satisfactorily answered by Mr Zhen, our English teacher who used to be a Russian interpreter in the railway bureau. My new acquisition of the Linguaphone course cheered me up a great deal, and I was taken, by the beautiful voices, to a world which was so amazingly different and so far away.

Teacher Lu, the English teacher for my sister Meiling's year, was better known among us pupils as Mr Donkey. As far as a nickname went, we all thought Mr Donkey was a brilliant invention. Apart from the fact that his surname sounded similar to the Chinese word for donkey, he always looked miserable, disapproving and sometimes was plain bad-tempered. In spite of his temper and miserable persona, he was considered to be a good linguist. I became really excited when Meiling told me that he was going to teach some extracurricular English in an after-school class. It was free, like all the after-school classes in our school at that time, and anyone who wanted to attend could do so, or so Mr Donkey said. One Saturday afternoon at the start of Mr Donkey's new course, I went along with Meiling, who took me on the rear seat of my father's old bicycle, which had lately started to become quite noisy. My mother's Russian bicycle, in not much better condition, was being used by Yan, who now worked at the railway station after my mother had finally taken the plunge and retired. The classroom had started to fill up when Mr Donkey, a short man in his late forties, came in with a half-smoked cigarette in his hand. He dropped on to the podium, quite unceremoniously, a few books he had under his left arm. Clearing his throat, he started to set up rules for his class. No chatting and no eating in class, he said, and we all nodded as he took a last puff at his cigarette before stubbing it out on the floor.

'You need to go,' he suddenly shouted in his throaty voice. Everybody in the classroom turned around and looked in my direction. I was astonished at him pointing his finger at me, and could not work out why he had picked on me. 'You will be no good, and it will be a waste of my time,' he sneered with his finger still pointing at me. 'Have I made myself clear?' he lashed out. Obviously, he thought that I was not advanced enough to follow his teaching, as I was a year below all the other pupils in the class. 'But . . .' I tried to defend myself, and was promptly stopped by his barking.

Reluctantly, and with a deep sense of embarrassment, I packed my things in front of a silent class. I signalled to Meiling, who looked really angry with Mr Donkey, to stay on. 'You are not a true teacher,' I mumbled to Mr Donkey as I left the classroom, but he totally ignored me. I was in tears when I got home.

'There is always one rotten apple in the basket.' My mother's comment about Mr Donkey put a smile on my face. That afternoon, she made me some Mongolian milk tea to cheer me up. Once again, I enjoyed this delightful drink made in the silver teapot that had once been used by her great-great-grandmother, except this time we no longer needed to worry about being tipped off and criticised any more.

If the term golden phoenix was invented for anybody, it had to be Miss Liang. I went to meet her one lunchtime at her parents' house, one of the yellow mud-rendered dwellings in the Peoples' Commune near us. I knew the compound well; Zhuji's parents, from whom my family had bought our 'dry' ducklings some years ago, lived there. I had heard that Miss Liang, a new graduate from a teacher training college, taught in a top middle school in our city which had an impressive number of leavers getting university places, which was very difficult at the time. Although our middle school was a good one, it was the consensus in our city that the railway bureau's schools were generally not as competitive as those under the municipal government.

I became really nervous when I reached the red front door of the Liangs' home. My heart beat very fast, and I stopped with my hand in the air just as I was about to knock on the door. I began to question whether I should have been there at all. After all, we didn't know Miss Liang, though I had seen her around. My fear of being rejected, after my experience with Mr Donkey, overtook me and I was just about to turn away from the door when a voice stopped me. In front of me stood a tall, slender and elegant young woman with almond eyes and rosy cheeks. She looked stunning in a pretty flower-patterned dress, and I felt like an ugly duckling. She asked me why I was there, and I explained that I desperately needed somebody who could answer the questions my teacher Mr Zhen could not. 'I would only come occasionally,' I said, trying not to be too much of a nuisance. A little intrigued by my request, she started to ask me questions in English such as where did I live and which year I was in at school. She then paused, and then hesitated for a while before she said, 'No problem,' with a smile.

A magpie flew over me and landed in a tree in the compound of the People's Commune as I was leaving. 'I will have good luck,' I thought to myself. As soon as the thought entered my head, I began to laugh at myself for starting to believe in such superstition. But for once, I hoped that the symbolism would work, because I knew that I needed all the luck I could get to realise my dream. I wanted to go to university, and I wanted to go soon.

II

Too Thin to Serve the Country

We were on the stage of the newly expanded and very impressive Railway Workers' Club. As the biggest employer in our city, with some tens of thousands of people in its workforce, the railway bureau had not stinted in doing up the club, a combined theatre, cinema and conference venue. I was conducting No. 1 Middle School's choir in a music competition on the National Day to mark the founding of the People's Republic.

I saluted to the audience and then announced the titles of our songs. To the applause of some two thousand people, I turned around to the choir. I lifted the baton in my right hand as I signalled the musicians in the pit to start. I felt great on the stage, and my new flower dress, which my mother had just finished sewing a couple of days earlier, also made me feel quite good about myself.

Our singing of 'Do-Re-Mi' was a hit and the audience applauded for a long time. Amid much applause, we started 'The Lonely Goatherd', which brought about even more excitement in the audience, most of whom looked impressed by our good performances from *The Sound of Music*. The choir, a little overwhelmed by the response, sang happily and enthusiastically, with members almost ignoring the tempo in a few places, although I managed to recover the situation quite well. Being a conductor was quite a coveted role, which attracted considerable admiration and even envy. 'She only got it because of her sister Yan, and I am not even faintly interested in it,' I overheard Fang, a plump girl from my class, talking to some choir members before a rehearsal, with her head tipped back and her eyes cast sideways. Fang, like her art teacher mother Teacher Fu, liked to put on an air of superiority and even defiance at times. In fact, it was only a few days before that I had seen her mother canvassing Teacher Zhang for Fang to be given the conductor's job. To be fair, Fang was quite a good accordion player and she had long set her heart on becoming the lead player in the school band, a position my sister Yan had held until the previous year when she graduated.

Most of the fifty choir members were pupils from Teacher Zhang's class, and this was not purely a coincidence. Teacher Zhang, a competitive person herself, had always insisted that her class should not only do well academically, but must also shine in sports and music.

It was finally the moment of truth and the atmosphere became tense when the head of education in the railway bureau was to announce the winners. We, the choir, looked at each other nervously backstage when the head gave his usual speech before the announcement. 'Come on, come on,' my friend Hong, a lead singer, said as she listened impatiently to the rambling speech. Then came the end of the speech, and everybody was applauding, including the head of education himself, who looked quite pleased with his own delivery. 'The bronze goes to . . .' came the announcement. Oh, dear, our chances were getting slimmer, Hong looked at me nervously. And the silver didn't come our way either, and the choir looked despondent. 'And finally, No. 1 Middle School . . .' came the words we wanted to hear, and the choir burst into cheers. Madam Zhang looked really pleased when I handed over the gold cup to her and she joined in our celebration. I can still remember the exhilaration I had when I bowed to the audience. At that moment, I thought of the 'chopstick baton' my mother had used to teach me music, and for the first time, I thought I understood a little what my grandfather, who by now had passed away, had said about how music and art could enrich life.

The music competition was only one of the many competitions we had at that time. Apart from many exams, we also had competitions in nearly every subject in our school, whose atmosphere was more and more geared towards league tables and the annual university entrance exam. 'I don't know how Ming managed to do that,' Madam Guan said one day after the results of the very first entrance exam came out. 'Not just to have got a university place, but a place in a key university as well.' She shook her head in amazement. 'And also in Beijing,' she continued with a degree of admiration and envy. 'Only about two per cent of the entrants in our city have got a university place, you know,' she added in the tone which she often used when she thought she was enlightening us. Ming was the first person in our neighbourhood to get a university place and he was a real success story of the newly revived university entrance system. I was really impressed by the stories going round in our neighbourhood about how Ming had stayed up all night to do revision and how he had often skipped lunch so that he could study during his lunch breaks at work. Thinking about it, that was in fact quite the norm at that time, as a large number of entrants – the backlog generated by the eleven years' gap of no entrance exam – were the 'old' school leavers now working in factories, in the fields or serving in the barracks. My sister Jing was also busy juggling work with revision and was really disappointed with her failure to get a place when she sat the first entrance exam.

Although Yan succeeded my mother at the railway station, she could not get into my mother's old team, which was considered a good place to work and was therefore sought after. Instead, she became a ticket conductor at the station, working shifts. It was not as good as it could have been, but Yan was just happy to put her days of potato picking behind her. Like Jing, she was also hoping that she could win a university place one day.

Since her retirement, my mother now had more time to spend on cooking, a nice change to the days when she had to rush to get our meals ready before she went to work. And it seemed that whenever she was in a rush, the coal balls in our stove would apparently conspire against her and refuse to burn properly, so that she often had to go to work without having time to eat anything. There was no more of that now. One thing my mother had started to cook quite often lately was the 'hedgehog', an egg-sized bun in the shape of a hedgehog. Mixing and kneading a dough, similar to bread dough, with lukewarm water, she would then give it a long rest before transferring it on to a lightly floured board. She would then roll it into a long sausage shape before cutting it into tennis-ball-sized pieces, before rolling out each piece flat, ready for the filling of azuki beans, or *hongdou* (red beans) as we called them. To prepare the filling, mother used to soak some overnight before boiling them the next day. Once they were boiled thoroughly, she would mash them up, adding a generous amount of sugar. Putting a spoonful of filling into each pastry piece, she would then form the pastry into a hedgehog shape while sealing the edge of the pastry at the same time. She would then mould the edges a little and add a few small pieces of pastry to each one to give the appearance of spines. The bit I liked most was when she gave the hedgehog its two eyes, and I remember I was always quite amazed at how she managed to make each hedgehog look so vivid by simply adding two boiled red peas. The steamed hedgehogs were delicious to eat either on their own or as an accompaniment to a spicy and aromatic pork dish mother started to cook often.

Yuxiang rousi was a very popular dish, and although the name itself suggested something related to fish (it means fish-flavoured pork slices), there was actually no fish involved at all. I have never managed to get to the bottom of why the dish is so named, and, as always, there were many explanations and fascinating stories about it. When cooking this dish, my mother would first mix pork, cut into thin strips, with a little water and cornflour before adding finely chopped spring onions, ginger and garlic, a little soy sauce, vinegar, rice wine, sugar, salt and a splash of sesame oil. She would then leave this all in the mixing bowl for a few minutes while cutting a couple of red chillies, some bamboo shoots and a few pieces of pre-soaked *muer*, a dark Chinese fungus, into thin strips. She would then fry the pork in very hot oil, stir until a distinct fragrance appeared before adding the red chillies, bamboo shoots and *muer*. A good stir later, she would then add the sauce from the meat bowl to the wok, and give it all another good stir, until cooked. *Yuxiang rousi* was an excellent dish, packed with flavours.

Apart from expanding her repertoire, my mother also started to buy more walnuts and Chinese red dates. 'Walnuts are good for your brain,' she told me one day as she tried to crack a few for me with a pair of pliers. Meiling and I used to crack walnuts by putting a couple strategically between the door and the door frame and pulling the door shut. To be honest, this didn't do our doors much good, but we certainly enjoyed the walnuts. For once, Madam Guan took a leaf out of my mother's book, and also started to give No. 7 and No. 8 a lot of walnuts to eat. She even asked my mother to help No. 7 and No. 8 with their school work. That was quite a leap for Madam Guan who, only a few years before, had thought that all spiritual food, together with all learning, was a waste of time. I suppose she had simply moved with the times.

I cannot remember that my mother ever talked about missing her job, and, as far as I could see, she seemed to be quite happy in her retirement. She occasionally reminisced about her old job, and sometimes she would meet up with a couple of her former colleagues. Looking back, I would say that her retirement actually gave her the opportunity to enjoy life a little more, which she had been deprived of during years of working and being a lone parent. Lately, she had taken up painting, and sometimes would ask for tips from Meiling who had progressed a great deal since the days of our school posters and was now quite an accomplished amateur artist.

The university entrance exam became the hottest subject in our city, and I remember that there was an interesting story going around then. As the story went, in the days leading up to the first entrance exam, the education ministry of China suddenly realised that they had got a problem coping with the sheer volume of people entering the exams. The problem was quite simply that they would not have enough paper to print all the exam papers for about six million entrants. This shortage of paper threatened to sabotage this momentous event for the country and for its millions of people. According to reports, Deng Xiaoping, one of China's great leaders, stepped in and made an incisive decision. Instead of continuing to print the fifth volume of the collected works of Chairman Mao, which was in progress at the time, the printers were instructed to give priority to the printing of the exam papers. And that decision saved the day.

Meiling was at a bit of crossroads at the age of fifteen. On

TOO THIN TO SERVE THE COUNTRY

the one hand, she wanted to pursue her dream of becoming a professional artist, while, on the other hand, the sciences beckoned. Encouraged by her art teacher Yang – a promising young artist who had brightened our city's scenery by doing some brilliant film and theatre advertisements outside the new Railway Workers' Club – Meiling started to produce some remarkable works. 'Don't move; stay in that position,' she used to say to me when I posed for her while doing my homework, of which we started to have more and more. Meiling would often rush to finish her homework so that she could start some painting.

Then came the day when she set off for Beijing to take the entrance exam to the art school affiliated to the Central Academy of Fine Arts, the top art establishment in China. It is perhaps worth mentioning that it was already a considerable achievement for her to have got this far, since she was one of only two finalists chosen out of three hundred or so applicants from Inner Mongolia to compete in Beijing with other finalists selected from other parts of the country, based on the portfolio of works she had sent to the school's examination board. Art and music operated a little differently at that time from the mainstream subjects, and the Central Academy's art school was *the* place to be for aspiring artists, and competition was stiff. I seem to recall hearing that several hundred applicants were competing for thirty or so places.

I still remember the day when the letter arrived from the art school. After a period of anxious waiting, our postman brought the news. Nervously, Meiling opened the official brown envelope. There was absolute silence as I watched her unfold, with trembling hands, the thin piece of letter-headed paper which would determine her future. Then, as if the light had been taken away from her usually bright almond eyes, her face fell and she silently passed the letter to me. It was not the good news we had hoped for. 'You did well to get in the finals,' I tried to comfort a disappointed Meiling. 'But that means nothing. Either you've won a place or you haven't,' she said with tears in her eyes, and her silent tears spoke of deep disappointment and confusion as to where to go next. The news that the art school would not be taking on any students from our area in the coming year did little to help her, and deep down, I knew that she was starting to feel quite worried about her future. It was the art school's policy then to rotate its recruitment, seen as an effective way of utilising its limited resources and also to give art school hopefuls in different areas, particularly in remote areas, a fair chance to compete for the small number of places. With my mother's job already having been passed on to Yan, getting a university place seemed to be the only option for Meiling to get anywhere in life. With only two years to go before she was due to finish middle school, she now needed to pull out all the stops and concentrate on her schoolwork if she wanted to win a university place in a mainstream subject. One day she told me that she had made up her mind to stop painting. I really didn't know what to say at the time, except to feel terribly sorry for her. 'I don't really mind,' she said to me, trying to make light of it. But I knew that she really did mind, a great deal.

Since Miss Liang had taken me on, I had made good progress with my English. While being conscious of keeping my promise to visit her only occasionally, I made the most of each of my visits by bombarding her with lengthy lists of questions that I had accumulated in between. She never seemed to mind, and it often seemed to me that she enjoyed the challenge.

'What's wrong with waiting for three years and then going to do mathematics at Qinghua?' Teacher Zhang said adamantly, and she didn't look very happy with me for raising the matter for the second time. As if she had already mapped out my future of studying at a top university, she continued, 'I know you are good enough to do it,' and her big eyes were fixed on me, with high expectations.

It was the beginning of the autumn term, the first of the two terms in the academic year. I had come to Teacher Zhang for the second time to ask for her approval for me to take a year of 'secondment' from my class in the third form to join a class in the fifth form, the highest form in our school. My plan was to learn in that one year all the subjects I needed to learn and revise all the things I needed to know, so that I could take part in the university entrance exam in the following summer . It was extremely unusual to 'leapfrog' two years in the middle school in order to take the university entrance exam earlier, and in fact, it had never been done in my school before. It would be extremely difficult, everybody had warned me, including my mother who had finally decided to go along with my plan after much persuasion from me. 'You can always do the third form again if it doesn't work out,' my mother said. 'It will work out,' I said with the confidence and dogged determination of a single-minded young girl. Looking back, I was like a child in a sweet shop, and the sheer promise of having something later was no longer enough. I wanted to go to university and I wanted to do it *now*.

'Want to get a university place to study English in Beijing?' sneered Mr Donkey one day, after he had seen me in the fifth form. 'Well, well, so here is our exceptional pupil, the one in a hundred.' A smirk swept over his face, which only made me feel more determined. After some persuasion, Teacher Zhang had agreed to release me, but with a strong warning that if I failed to get a university place, which was more likely than not, given the overall success rate, it would be unlikely that I would then be able to catch up with my peers in the third form and I would miss out, particularly in sciences. 'But I can do both sets of courses,' I said. 'If you can't decide between two boats, you'll fall into the water,' she reminded me of an old saying, but for the moment at least she decided to indulge me.

Madam Ran, a kind history teacher in her early fifties, took me into her class in the fifth form, and she did it without much persuasion. Looking back, I think that she was not only intrigued by my case, which the school had not seen before, but also keen to take on a challenge. The sound of my heavy wooden desk chair knocking on the concrete staircases now became a feature in the school building during breaks, while I was trying to combine attending science lectures in the third form with doing history and geography lessons in the fifth form. For a university place to study English, I needed to do history, geography, Chinese language and maths papers as well as English and political studies. My green canvas bag was bursting with books, and my brain sometimes felt as though it was bursting too.

'You have to make up your mind now,' Teacher Zhang called me to her office one day. The two-month period of indulgence was over, and she wanted me to decide one way or another. With reluctance, I told her that I wanted to concentrate on English, humanities and maths for the entrance exam in the following year, and therefore would give up my place in her class, for which there was already a queue. Teacher Zhang looked disappointed. 'Why English? At best, you will only end up being a language teacher,' she said unequivocally, in a last effort to try to steer me back to the sciences, in which she believed I would excel. I remember I felt really sad, sadder than I had ever thought that I would be, when I left behind the heavy wooden chair which had shared so much joy in sciences with me, thanks to a brilliant teacher.

'Decided to burn your boats, then?' Mr Zhen, our English teacher, said to me during the mid-morning break one day soon after I had left Teacher Zhang's class. I was chatting to a few friends at the sports ground where we had just had our morning exercises, a daily routine in which all the pupils did, in groups, a set of exercises, mostly stretching ones, to the rhythm of the radio music. I nodded, with a faint smile and some trepidation, to Mr Zhen, who was a tall and impressive-looking man. To many of us in school, he always came across as being incredibly sophisticated, incisive and above all, wise, perhaps because of his upbringing in a wealthy industrialist family in 1920s Shanghai, or so I had heard on the grapevine. Even though he could not fully explain some of the grammar-related questions I had now, my high regard for him and his opinions remained intact. 'In that case, you'd better carry on as the ancient soldiers then,' Mr Zhen said with an avuncular smile, referring to an old Chinese story about a famous general who, around 200 BC, had burned the boats after his soldiers had crossed a river on their way to fight the enemy. Mr Zhen's remark brought home to me just what a gamble I might be taking and, for the first time since I had left Teacher Zhang's class, I felt really worried and nervous about my decision. My doubts, however, didn't last long, and I soon regained my composure, confidence and self-belief. Almost as if I, too, had crossed a river of no return, I simply became even more determined.

My new class in the fifth form greeted me with considerable curiosity. They were used to having university hopefuls joining them from time to time, and in fact, a couple of twenty-year-olds who had left the school two years earlier, had recently rejoined the class because they had failed the university entrance exams. But the class, on average seventeen to eighteen years old, were simply not used to having somebody younger than them in their midst. To some sceptical people, I was simply a fourteen-year-old living in a fantasy world, or even a toad lusting after swan meat, as we used to say in our city about somebody chasing something too ambitious or perhaps even something that they were unworthy of. 'She won't last long, just too much to catch up with,' a maths teacher gave me an embarrassed smile when I overheard him agreeing with Teacher Fu in the school corridor. In a way he was right, and, apart from revision, I also had to cram into one year what the others had learned over two years.

The red rubber ball was magical. At the suggestion of Mr Wang, the inspirational geography teacher, my mother had bought me a large rubber ball, a cheap alternative to buying a globe. Almost instantly, the world was, literally, in my hands, and the time-zone calculation, which I had had something of a problem with at the beginning, became really easy. Whenever I asked Mr Wang, a thin man in his late twenties, questions, which I often did, he would always patiently explain. Most of the time, though, instead of giving me a direct answer to my question, he would challenge me to think hard for myself. I can still remember his small, kind eyes smiling encouragingly, behind his black thick glasses, the type of glasses which seemed to be the thing to have in our city at that time. It was not easy; in fact, it was very hard work to catch up, to learn new things and to revise at the same time. I had to make the most of every waking hour, and my days normally started at six in the morning and finished somewhere around eleven at night. 'I'm going to switch off the light now,' Meiling, who took it upon herself to make sure I had enough sleep, often felt the need to step in. 'Just one last page,' I used to negotiate with her.

Lately, some teachers had started to promote revision-aid books, most of which were, I recall, compiled by experienced teachers of some considerable fame. I used to look down at my desk when the teachers were promoting them, as I felt a little uneasy for not responding to their recommendations. Not that I didn't respect their recommendations, I simply didn't want to ask my mother to dip into our family's limited finances to buy those normally quite expensive books. 'Don't forget to take some money for your book,' my mother said one lunchtime when I was engrossed in a new revision aid that I had borrowed from Dongmei, a kind and generous girl. In spite of their initial curiosity, and perhaps reservations, many of my new classmates in the fifth form soon took to me, and to some extent, they indulged me like a little sister. On more than one occasion, the head boy in charge of the classroom cleaning rota let me off cleaning the classroom even though it was my turn. Dongmei, in particular, took me under her wing and, whenever there was even a mild joke about my being small and young, she leapt to my defence like a lioness. 'No need,' I mumbled to my mother to say that I didn't want to buy the book because it was not particularly useful. 'We can afford books, you know,' my mother said cheerfully, as if she were a millionairess. Looking back, I don't know how my mother managed to keep cheerful in the face of all our difficulties and adversities, and the truth is that I didn't want her to make yet more sacrifices. Besides, I had the indulgence of some of my classmates who would kindly allow me to read their revision aids, but only, understandably, during the breaks when they were not using them. I was really pleased with that arrangement and would delve into the books at tremendous speed whenever I had the opportunity, even though it meant I sometimes skipped lunch.

My sister Yan was also busy preparing for what would be her

third attempt to get into university. She wanted to get a place in the music department of the teacher training college in our city. Like art courses, music operated a little differently from the mainstream subjects. First, she needed to pass what was called the speciality test, which in her case was accordion playing and music theory. Then, once she had passed that, she needed to sit exams in the humanities in the university entrance exam. It was not so easy for Yan to combine working at the railway station with preparation for exams, but at least she had an advantage this time – she could borrow my revision notes and even get a few tips from me. Thinking about it now, it must have been quite difficult for her to get help from her little sister, more than five years younger. Occasionally, I recall, there seemed to be a despondency in her eyes, which was not helped by her previous failures.

It must have been the adrenalin at work, for I cycled down the low bridge to our school at a record speed. It was just half an hour to the closing of the enrolment for the entrance exam when I got to the school, and a crowd of entrants were still busy making the last alterations to their application forms, which could not be changed once the enrolment was closed. 'Think before you put pen to paper,' Madam Ran was telling off a girl who had made a mess of her form as she kept altering her choices of university and the order of her choices. 'Be realistic and be sensible,' Madam Ran was now addressing all the entrants, who all looked pretty stressed, as they were about to make a potentially life-changing decision based on their predictions of their own results in the imminent entrance exam. 'Be logical, and concentrate on making the right first choice in the key and non-key university categories,' she continued, trying to help the crowd sort out their applications in time. 'An unsuitable first choice would not only make you lose the opportunity to go to your chosen university, it could also ruin your chance of being taken by your second choice. Let's face it, all universities are going to give priority to people who have put them down as their first choice,' she added firmly. As I tried to get to the teacher in charge of all the application forms, I nodded in agreement. I wished that somebody had given this advice to Jing, who had found out, to her cost, that some entrants with lower scores than her in the first entrance exam, had been offered places by a university which had rejected her because she had not put it as her first choice.

I rushed back to retrieve my form and correct the mistake I thought I might have made with my own choices. Earlier on, I had handed in my form, relatively happy with my decision of selecting a key university in our city as my first choice, endorsed by my mother who had said the university had a good reputation. As one of the national key universities, the highest status of university category, it was indeed well recognised. The remoteness of our city, however, did make it less attractive compared to universities of the same status in Beijing. Since our city was far from desirable to most strong entrants from other parts of the country, many of my school friends thought this would be a safe option, and I had chosen to play safe as well. I was shaking as I tried to fish my application form out of hundreds of forms, now fast piling up as the deadline approached rapidly. I now began to feel really annoyed with myself for having played safe earlier on, and for having almost abandoned my dream of returning to Beijing, a city I had fallen in love with during my first visit there some years before. I was relieved to find my form and quickly changed my first choice to a Beijing university, just in time.

A month or so passed and the day now finally arrived. It was a hot July day, the first of the three days over which the annual entrance exam took place. As I reached the examination venue, one of many in our city, I was greeted by a few policemen who had been guarding the site against any possible leak of the exam papers or any other possible fraudulent behaviour. In the morning sun, I walked through a pair of tall iron gates and I could feel behind me the gaze of my mother, who was among hundreds of other anxious parents. Earlier that morning I had actually been a little sick with pre-exam nerves, and the sight of an ambulance parked near the gates made me feel a little uncomfortable. A glance around the exam hall showed that there were many worried faces, and the atmosphere was so tense that one could almost cut it with a knife. My nerves, somehow, took a dramatic turn for the better as soon as we were told to start on the papers. All the anxiety and worry suddenly seemed to disappear, and to my intense relief, I became calm and focused.

My calm was not to last, and I was sick again over lunch in front of the delicious cuttlefish, fragrant rice and fried bean curd, my favourite food, specially cooked by Jing, who had taken a few days off from her studies at a polytechnic in a nearby city. Having failed twice in the entrance exam, she finally won a place at the age of 22 on her third attempt, one year before mine. She was disappointed not to get into a proper university, but was pleased that she did at least have a chance to further herself. Jing made a special clear mung bean soup, said to help reduce the negative impact of the summer heat, and she tried her very best to entice me to eat it. But I didn't have any appetite for it, or, indeed, for anything else. Anxious that I should eat something before facing more exam papers in the afternoon, my mother and Jing racked their brains as to what to do when I had a sudden hankering for fried eggs and tomatoes. My mother sped off on her bicycle to search for some tomatoes, but it was a mammoth task. With tomatoes only starting to come on to the market, as the tomato season always started late in our city because of the climate, my mother cycled, at break-neck speed, to many stalls and street markets, pressed by the limited time before I had to return to the exam venue. I recall that she rushed in with a few tomatoes, mostly green, which she quickly passed to Jing who had them washed, cut and cooked in no time. I can still remember the pleasure in their faces as they watched me tucking in, but that was not to last either, and it was not long before I was sick again. To our great relief, the exam paper in the afternoon, just as in the morning, seemed to have the effect of curing my sickness, and I felt perfectly normal when I did the paper. The next two days followed more or less the same pattern, with my nerves playing tricks and Jing being tested to the limit with her cooking.

'Don't move, and stand still on the scale,' a thin, thirty-some-thing said behind her white mouth-mask, which most doctors wore in our city when seeing patients. 'Stay there.' She frowned a little as she took another close look at the reading before writing down my weight. I was in one of the city's biggest hospi-tals, receiving a full medical check-up, a prerequisite for all university hopefuls. 'Everything OK?' I asked, having now nearly come to the end of my check-up. 'No, it's not, You're too thin,' she said matter-of-factly as she scribbled some comments on my form. 'But I am three years younger than the others, and I'll grow and get bigger,' I pleaded for her not to write down any negative comment, which could just end my university dream there and then. 'I'm not so sure, 36 kilos is very light, even for your age,' she continued. She then hesitated a little before taking my form away. I followed her, to her obvious annoyance, and she slammed the door shut in my face as she got to the office of the head of her department. I ran to find my mother who was waiting for me at the reception, and having heard about my light weight, she marched straight into the very office where the two doctors were now in the middle of deciding on my fate. Mustering up some extraordinary strength, she delivered a passionate and impromptu plea to the two doctors. My mother mentioned the food shortages we had all gone through, and the difficult circumstances in which I had grown up. 'We need to exercise common sense when we are involved in such a life changing decision,' she said passionately, and she pleaded them to look at my weight in the context of my age, rather than simply checking it against the guideline tables.

Her persuasion worked, and the senior doctor nodded to my mother as he instructed his junior colleague to cross out the comment that I was 'too thin to serve the country' before he put the rubber stamp of his department near the alteration to make the correction valid. As we walked out of the office of the senior doctor, both my mother and I took a long and deep breath.

The exam results finally came in late summer, and I had achieved better results than I had predicted. 'You'll definitely go to Beijing,' Madam Ran said authoritatively after looking at my result sheet. 'Amazingly good overall scores, far above the entry threshold for non-key universities and even considerably higher than the requirements for key universities,' she remarked. She then told me that I had achieved one of the highest overall scores out of over two hundred entrants from our school, which I later learnt, had done very well, with fifteen reaching the entry threshold, a success rate higher than the then national average. Teacher Zhang looked really pleased for me when I told her about my results. 'I still think, though, you'd make a good mathematician,' she could not resist the temptation to tell me for the last time.

The summer days post-exams were filled with anticipation

and also the sheer pleasure of having some free time at last. Many days were spent visiting friends and visiting yet more friends. Apart from meeting up with my 'new' classmates, such as Dongmei from the fifth form, I also had a lot to catch up with my 'old' friends from Teacher Zhang's class, many of whom came to congratulate me or even to get tips from me. Dongmei, in spite of having had poor results, looked genuinely pleased for me and she, like some other friends, arranged for us to have a picture taken together in a photo studio. Having a photo taken together in a studio, as a parting present, was still quite a fashionable thing to do in Huhehot in the early 1980s, as very few people had their own cameras. Since the exams, I had also been busy sorting out my clothes. Busy was perhaps an exaggeration, as I didn't exactly have that many clothes. With the few pieces of clothing I had though, I went through them with the same attachment as one would have to a Chanel little black number or an Yves St Laurent trouser suit. I was simply trying to decide what attire I should adopt for Beijing. 'What clothes have we packed for Beijing today, then?' Yan used to tease me as I kept moving my pile of clothes from one corner of the bedroom to another as if I knew I was definitely going to Beijing. Although she was very disappointed with her poor result, which meant she had failed once again in her third attempt to get into university, she was really pleased for me.

It was a late summer afternoon, and our postman had already done his first delivery. I could not settle to anything, and kept looking out of the widow while helping Meiling with her English revision. Having guessed that my mind was on something else, she decided to switch to do her own revision in sciences, at which she excelled. With just about a year to go before taking the entrance exam, she was putting everything in. The familiar

167

sound of the postman's bicycle bell rang and I ran outside, like an Olympic contestant sprinting to the finishing line. Our postman always rang his bell when he had post for us, particularly when he knew we were expecting something important. Looking back, our reliable postman, in a unique way, had shared our joy, our hopes and at times our disappointments over those years. He had played an important, albeit unsung, role in that chapter of our life.

My hands trembled as our postman passed me the official-looking brown envelope addressed to me. 'So, little sister is our golden phoenix then,' he said smiling, as he got on his saddle, cheerfully ringing his bell as his way of saying goodbye. Meiling was by now at the front door, smiling at me with her bright almond eyes. I had never known that an envelope could be so difficult to open, and my hands shook like leaves as I opened the envelope, eagerly but carefully. My face must have said it all, and before I uttered a word, Meiling's eyes were filled with excitement and joy. Hardly did my mother have a chance to park her bicycle before I handed her my admission letter. I cannot recall what she said, or whether indeed she said anything. Her face said it all, and she looked so happy. We laughed when the tomatoes in her bicycle basket went rolling everywhere as her ill-parked bicycle collapsed to the ground. That day, we celebrated with four happiness, those delicious meatballs, and they had never tasted so good.

The news that I had got a place in a key university in Beijing excited our neighbours who were still talking about the 'amazing Ming' some three years after he had first gone to university in Beijing. 'A child prodigy,' our neighbour Madam Jiao shook her head with a degree of disbelief and amazement as she congratulated my mother, who smiled in her self-deprecating way. 'That is the second highest score in the whole of Inner Mongolia,'

Miss Liang exclaimed after she had learnt about my scores in English. Characteristically for her, my mother didn't go overboard with words of praise, but I could see in her eyes just how pleased she was, and so were my sisters. In fact, we had not been so happy for a very long time.

12

Peking Duck and University Challenge

'Hey, you,' a security guard tapped me on the shoulder from the back. I turned around to see a stern-looking man in his twenties. 'Who gave you permission to talk to the foreigners?' he asked me with a face cold as sub-zero. The appearance of the security guard soon prompted the gathering of a bigger crowd.

I was at the People's Department Store, a major store in our city, getting the last few things I needed just a couple of days before I set off for Beijing to start my university life. While I was shopping with my mother, I saw a foreign couple, in their late twenties or early thirties, trying to communicate with some of the shop assistants in a mixture of Chinese, English and sign language amid endless stares and many curious onlookers. It was still rare in our city to see foreigners, and in fact they were the first European-looking people I had ever come close to. I was very tempted to speak English to native speakers for the first time, and I looked at my mother who smiled at me encouragingly. 'Excuse me, can I help you?' I said in textbook English, quite nervously, anxious to see whether they could in fact understand me. So far, apart from speaking English to my uncle, my English teachers at No. 1, Miss Liang and a small panel of examiners at the entrance exam's orals, I had spoken largely to myself and to the Friesian cows. After a short pause, which had perhaps been triggered by surprise, the couple looked at me with delight and kindness which soon put me at ease. We got chatting and they told me that they were newly married and were from England. As we were talking, the wife, a gentle and pretty lady, skilfully drew me a map of Britain on the back of an envelope and showed me where they came from. Going through her handbag quickly, the lady was keen to find something English to give me as a memento. My confidence grew as our conversation meandered, and all the sentences and phrases I had learnt from Voice of America and the Linguaphone course suddenly came alive. Our conversation attracted a lot of attention from customers, most of whom did not seem to mind at all that they were not being served by the many shop assistants who had also stopped to watch. It always surprised me that this store often seemed to have more staff than customers, although this was quite the norm in our city at that time.

The appearance of the security guard intrigued the English couple a little at first, but they soon started to look quite baffled as the guard became somewhat aggressive. 'Just tell them you have to go, and say nothing else,' the guard ordered me, as I attempted to explain to the couple what was going on. I was left with no choice but to bring my conversation with the nice couple to an abrupt end before I was taken to the Party Secretary's office, alone.

The Party Secretary of the store, a middle-aged Mongolian man, did not look particularly interested as the guard reported on my transgression. 'What conversation could a little one like you have with foreigners?' he asked in Chinese with a strong Mongolian accent. 'I am not little, I am a university student,' I challenged him. He laughed and mumbled something to a woman colleague in whom he showed far more interest. 'She, a university student,' she said, shaking her head in disbelief while, after taking a puff at his cigarette, he signalled the guard to take me out of his office. 'Don't talk to strangers any more, particularly not foreigners.' He waved his cigarette-stained fingers in the air. 'They might be imperialist spies,' he added with a sigh, just before I was taken away. It seemed that what was worrying him more was not the fact that I might have broken some foreign-affairs rules, as the guard had accused me of, but my state of mind in fantasising that I was a much-envied university student. As I was cheerfully leaving the office, the guard, having lost face a little because of the lack of interest from the Party Secretary, demanded that I hand over the magazine cutting the English couple had given me. It was a photo of the future Princess of Wales. Thinking about it now, I can almost still remember the kind and happy faces of the English couple. Wherever they are now, I wish them well. I only wish I could have explained to them why I had to end our conversation so abruptly.

Beijing greeted me, once again, with a beautiful sunny day. It was just as I remembered it, except that it looked even more colourful, more vibrant and more interesting. I arrived in Beijing with my black 'coffin', the nickname given by my fellow students to the big heavy black trunk which made me famous on my first day on the campus. I had inherited this big trunk from my cousin Shengli, and he had proudly made it out of hard wood in his days as a worker-peasant-soldier student. Now a lecturer in one of our city's universities and a married man, he felt he was ready to pass this huge object to me. To be honest, I had had some doubts about using the trunk, but I didn't feel that I had much choice. With my mother already having to buy various things for me before the start of my university life, I didn't want her to spend even more on a suitcase. Since her retirement, our family finances had become a little more stretched, as Yan's salary was not quite enough to fill the gap between my mother's previous salary and her pension. Seeing the sleek and expensive-looking suitcases that some of my classmates had, I was quite tempted to disown my trunk or simply to hide behind it, and it was certainly big enough for me to do so. But my embarrassment was pretty short-lived, and it was soon swallowed up by the excitement and laughter on the campus.

The canteen was always one of the liveliest places. Amidst the clicking sound of the bowls, mostly enamelled, there were often debates going on, in different dialects, no less varied and no less entertaining than those of my cousins' circle who used to bring fun and delicious cooking to our small house so many years ago. Sometimes, the debates in the canteen would take place in different languages, with quite a few language students keen to practise or just to show off. It was a stimulating place, with some of the best brains from all parts of the country involved in all sorts of discussions and airing all sorts of views. 'Very Beijing-like, they talk as if they know about the next government reshuffle even before it is announced,' Lei, a thin, bright-eyed Shanghai man said one day, a little sarcastically, in the queue when a few students were debating loudly, once again about politics, quite a trade-mark of Beijingers. 'All you smart Shanghainese are inter-ested in is making money,' Cheng, a tall, broad-shouldered man from Beijing snapped back. Cheng's riposte seemed to have united the debating party and they all cheered at his remark. My earlier training in various dialects and accents soon endeared me to some Shanghai students who were intrigued that I could in fact understand quite a bit of their supersonic talking. Sometimes, they would tease me and ask me to interpret into *Putonghua* some jokes told in Shanghai dialect, which at times resulted in some hilarious misunder-standings that had everyone in stitches.

The menu could sound just as interesting as some of the

debates. Ants climbing trees, phoenix feet, lion's head and pig's trotters were regularly being featured on the menu written out on a big blackboard in the kitchen. I had never heard of ants climbing trees before, and my first taste of it, I recall, was amid a heated debate about its origins, which had been triggered by my question. Made with minced pork, each small piece of meat was said to be an ant climbing among a nest of ground mung-bean vermicelli that was the trees, and it was quite delicious, particularly if with a touch of spice. After my first taste of it, I chose to have ants climbing trees quite often, though at times I was rather disappointed that there seemed to be too many trees and not enough ants. Apart from its flavour, I chose it because it was relatively cheap. As in other universities at that time, our canteen food was quite heavily subsidised, but I was still keen to save so that I could get by on my grant without having to ask my mother for help. I was lucky to get both of the types of grant available, with one being based on family financial circumstances and the other based on academic results. My treat to myself was always lion's head, a dish I had liked ever since Uncle Deng first cooked it for us some years before. It was a popular dish with many students, and sometimes when I had my mind set on it for lunch, I would be very disappointed if the chefs didn't include it on the menu or, even worse, if I was too late in the queue. Lion's head was always worth waiting for, with its lovely meatballs and delicious sauce, but, no matter how good it was, it never seemed to quite match the one cooked by Uncle Deng.

'Poppet, still hard at it?' Jiuhong from Year 4, the final year, said to me one day in her usual operatic voice in our communal wash room. I was in the middle of clothes washing, which I had been doing for some time now. In our four-storey block of dormitories, there were two wash rooms on each floor, with each shared by about six dormitories. Jiuhong was a big, tall girl of about 24, who could come across as quite direct, authoritative or even a little fierce to many people. She was never like that to me though, and in fact there was often a smile on her pretty, rounded face when she saw me, reminiscent of somebody reunited with a favourite doll. In fact, she sometimes called me a doll, like some others in her year, and quite a few of them were in their late twenties. They were what we called in my home city the 'old' school leavers, part of the backlog generated by the years when there were no entrance exams during the Cultural Revolution. Sometimes, I found it quite amusing when I heard Jiuhong and her friends talking about their factories and villages, but in fact, it was quite the norm then to have students in the third or fourth year who had either worked in factories or farmed in the fields before their university days. Although a little embarrassing at times, I didn't generally mind being called a poppet or a doll as being friends with students in the upper years, I felt, gave me a certain amount of street cred. To say the least, having carte blanche to visit Jiuhong and her friends in their dormitories at any time was a pretty impressive thing to have achieved. 'You can borrow anything you like from us, including clothes,' one of Jiuhong's friends offered. 'That is, if you can find anything small enough to fit you,' she quickly added, because she soon realised that she could be teased for her offer.

Continuing with my washing, I nodded, with a faint smile and a little frustration, at Jiuhong. For some reason, washing looked so easy for others, but the wooden washboard, which my mother had used for years before its arrival on the campus with me, often seemed to be working against me. Not only did it take me longer to finish washing a piece of clothing, but also it never looked as clean as when my mother, Jing or Yan used to wash it for me – we did not have a washing machine at home, a luxury item at that time. The truth is that with hardly any experience in washing clothes, I struggled helplessly. The feeling of helplessness made me feel homesick, something I managed, most of the time, to conquer. The excitement of campus life normally helped me to overcome any homesickness, but whenever I felt a little weak, my mother's letters, always accompanied by a little note from Meiling, were a constant source of comfort – my mother didn't have a telephone then. I often put my mother's letters and Meiling's notes under my pillow and would read them again and again before I went to sleep. If and when I missed home, I tried my hardest not to show it.

Jiuhong came to the rescue this time. Having quite unceremoniously thrown away the water in my enamelled wash bowl, she put in a couple of handfuls of washing powder before pouring from her thermos flask some hot water into the bowl. With the powder nicely dissolved and with the lather forming, she put in some cold water from the tap and then finally put my grey jacket, which had been made out of one of my mother's old jackets, back into the bowl. 'Leave it to soak for a while before you do this –' she demonstrated with the washboard. 'Use my washboard, yours is hopeless,' she said in her no-nonsense style before marching off. I nodded with tears in my eyes, tears of gratitude mixed with tears of homesickness.

In spite of her directness, I liked Jiuhong a lot. I remember that I felt quite upset one day when I heard a couple of girls talking about her being fat because there was something wrong with her hormone balance. I didn't fully understand, at the age of 15, what hormone imbalance was all about but I had gathered, from the tone of their voices, that the two girls were not being exactly complimentary, so I avoided laughing at their joke at her expense. My lack of interest in their joke somewhat surprised the two girls before one of them said, in a rather irritating and patronising tone, 'Oh, she is too young to know anything.'

Such remarks sometimes upset me a little, and often spurred me to push myself really hard. One of the things we did in the PE class in the first term was gymnastics on parallel bars. Like political studies, PE was part of the curriculum for all students. In front of the high bars, I recall, I felt very small and simply helpless. Not only did my height not help, but my thin arms were in no way strong enough to allow me to do anything. Madam Lai, the PE teacher and a straight-talking ex-soldier, was not quite used to dealing with girls as small as I was. With PE classes, the boys and girls in our year did separate activities. 'Please show me again,' I asked Madam Lai once again in the hope that I could pick up any tricks which I might have missed. I watched, digested and practised, but no matter how hard I tried it still didn't work for me. It's so unfair, I thought to myself when I watched most of the girls in my year, including some who were not at all sporty, manage the gymnastics on the bars. It was not that I could not do the gymnastics part of the exercise, I simply could not get on to the bars, as they were too high for me. I felt really annoyed with myself, but cheered up a little when I thought of the days when I was among a small group of hopeful gymnasts. I recall that about ten of us, mostly eight or nine years old, had all stood straight in a line, with our legs and arms being examined critically and measured by a coach from the Inner Mongolia youth gymnastic team. It was part of the selection process for the team that competed nationally, and I still remember the excitement when I, in my shorts and a small top, waited for the coach to deliver his verdict. I was a possibility, he said with a smile, but only one boy in our group met his exacting standard. It was now the scoring time for the parallel bars. 'You can skip it if you like,' Madam Lai offered, sympathetically, after watching me struggle, to the suppressed laughter of some and the not-so-suppressed laughter of others. I acknowledged Madam Lai's offer but decided to do it nevertheless. Having taken a few seconds to focus, I mustered up all the energy I could and there I was, to the surprise of everybody including myself, doing the routine on the bars. There was a silence, followed by excited applause. Even the girl who had said I was imma-ture gave a thumbs-up in my direction.

'Leave me alone,' I said to Cheng, who, instead of getting annoyed, smiled behind his big glasses. Cheng, the enthusi-astic debater in the canteen, often sat next to me in class. There were 19 students in our English language class. Our timetable in the mornings tended to be dominated by specialist classes such as reading, listening comprehension and speaking, trans-lating and interpreting. Sometimes, we would also have lectures in the afternoon, mostly on general subjects such as history, Chinese language and politics, when we would often be joined by other language students in our year, specialising in other European languages.

Cheng was only trying to talk to me after he had seen me earlier on playing with the accordion he had borrowed from the students' union. In fact, we had been chatting about music quite a bit for some time. At first, I didn't mind that at all, and at times, I rather enjoyed our chats, as he was quite a reasonable accordion player. But lately I had started to become a little embarrassed when he chatted to me, largely because of the teasing going on in our class and the rumours that Cheng fancied me. I had in fact gone out of my way to try to avoid him, and that also seemed to have generated some comment. Thinking about it now, at the age of 15 or so, I was indeed not as interested in boys as were the other five girls in my class, who were all about three years older than me. Instead, I much enjoyed the company of Chaucer, Shakespeare, Dickens, Thomas Hardy, the Brontë sisters, Jane Austen and D. H. Lawrence, and I was often absorbed in their green and pleasant land with its beautiful mountains and clouded hills.

The library became one of my much-loved haunts. It was not only a place to satisfy my hunger for knowledge, but it soon became apparent there that my love for corned beef might be indulged more easily as well. It was not until recently that I had become friends with Ruiyun, a gentle soul and a fellow language student in my year, who also frequented the library. One day, on our way back from the library, Ruiyun suggested that instead of going to the canteen, perhaps we could make our own supper together. 'Making' was a bit of an exaggeration, but I jumped at the idea. Armed with a couple of bags of instant noodles, which became quite popular among the students, we bought a tin of corned beef and a couple of tomatoes. I loved corned beef, but I rarely bought it on my own, as it was quite expensive and would stretch my monthly budget too much. Over our discussion about *Jane Eyre*, a film of which we had recently watched and both loved, we shared the delicious corned beef, carefully sliced with my father's fruit knife, which was much like a miniature Swiss army knife. The beef was complimented by our sliced tomatoes sprinkled with sugar and the spicy noodles instantly made with hot water. It was the start of many of our corned beef suppers together, and Ruiyun often indulged me, like a big sister, by letting me have the last slice of meat.

'Why don't *you* go out with him then?' I said to Qian, a plump girl in my class, one day, quite irritated by her constant interest and interference. I sensed an ulterior motive in her allegedly helping to 'build a bridge between Cheng and me', and it seemed that she just wanted an excuse to get close to him herself. 'No need to be like that.' Qian looked embarrassed, looking down and blushing. She blushed quite often, particularly in front of boys. Thinking about it now, I suppose I did lash out at her, perhaps a little unnecessarily. It was not that I really minded if she wanted to go out with Cheng, I had simply just had enough of her phoney helpfulness. Besides, I was probably just taking the opportunity to get back at her a little. She had irritated me for some time now, and as one of my five roommates sharing a one-room dormitory, she had constantly made fun of my small collection of clothes and my big black trunk. At the beginning of each term, she would often be in her element, passing around her goody bag, normally filled with delicious snacks brought back from her home near Xian. She always had an interesting way of passing things around, and as it happened, I always seemed to end up being the last one to be offered or the one whom she forgot 'by accident' every time. 'That looks a bit funny,' she would say and make a face when I offered her in return some of my limited supplies, which were probably not as expensive as hers but were nevertheless still precious to me. The fact of the matter was that with my home city not being renowned for good snacks and with my family being short of money, I was simply not an interesting proposition for her. It did not take long for me to start leaving the dormitory when she started her round, or, if it was too late to leave, I would pretend that I was so fully engaged with something else that I could not possibly take any of her offering after all. Thankfully, her behaviour was not universally popular, and her scheme normally fell flat on its face, when the other girls rarely showed much interest in tasting her food and barely volunteered anything in return.

'That's not peeling, that's slaughtering,' Yu, a Beijing girl with an oval face and long eyes resembling an ancient Chinese beauty, exclaimed one day as she watched me peeling, with my father's blue fruit knife, a juicy pear. She was keen to demonstrate to me the 'proper' way to peel a pear, as she said, and as soon as I passed her the fruit knife and the pear, she could not wait to show off. She was really good at it, though, and watching her slender hands moving with amazing dexterity was a treat to the eyes. Yu, who lived in an adjacent dormitory, often came to our dormitory to chat and I liked her a lot, because she was friendly, helpful and very funny. For a girl of 18, she had an amazing collection of tales to entertain us, most of which, she told us, came from her father, the editor of a large newspaper. She was also terribly good at mimicking people and, even as she skilfully peeled my pear, she was mimicking, vividly, two students from Guangdong bargaining with the fruit vendors in a nearby stall earlier on.

'This is a young, small bloom about to blossom,' Zuo, the self-proclaimed 'philosopher' of our class declared one day in front of the whole class, to the cheers of the boys and the giggles of the girls. Zuo, a small, self-assured man, liked to create a bit of drama in our class. Sometimes he would come to the class declaring that he had been just enlightened by Napoleon, his hero, and he even bought himself a pair of knee-length boots, so that he could look more like his hero. All the attention turned to me, the subject of his remark. I blushed a little, but secretly felt really pleased, particularly with the new jacket and trousers my roommate Min had just bought for me in Shanghai. Lately, I started to feel pretty good about myself, partly because of my newly gained weight, thanks largely to the canteen food. It had been a while now since Min, a slim, trendy and sophisticated Shanghai girl, had taken on the job of buying clothes for me in Shanghai during the two holidays we had every year. Although there was by now more widespread movement of goods around the country, the market in any particular city was still largely dominated by locally made goods. As far as clothing was concerned, Shanghai definitely beat Beijing in terms of style and fashion, while my home city came towards the bottom. I had always had a fondness for things made in Shanghai, as my very few memories of my father often seemed to have some-thing to do with the beautiful things he had brought back from his business trips to the south. Recently, I had also started wearing lipstick, which made me feel pretty and quite grown-up. I still remember the excitement I had on seeing my very first lipstick that my mother had bought me in our home city. 'Just use a little bit every time,' she said, as she showed me, gently and carefully, the magic green tube. It was unthinkable even a few years earlier that I could have had lipstick, as wearing make-up had then been considered to be decadent.

Campus life was by no means all work and no play. With ballroom dancing much in vogue in China, our canteen was the ideal place for girls and boys to meet up for a waltz and tango on weekend evenings when the dining tables were all neatly piled up to make room for weekend night fever. I was no longer shy of the attention of the boys, and truly loved the dancing which was often followed by parties in the dormitories. Obviously the parties with the most delicious night snacks and food on offer were more popular, and wonton soup was one of the favoured foods. Although some boys liked to indulge in drinking, mostly beer and *baijiu*, a strong liquor, clear and colourless like gin but with a much stronger taste, drinks never seemed to be a big thing at those parties, except for a few bottles of Beijing beer or a few tins of the famous Qingdao beer. There seemed to be quite a bit of competition between different party organisers to see who could come up with the best food. I was always quite amazed at how good some of the boys were at cooking. With no kitchen facilities in our dormitories, the food was mostly cooked on a single electrical ring, which constantly resulted in the power being cut off over the weekend because the fuse had blown. This didn't seem to deter many people, and as hard as the university tried to stop us, the cooking went on. 'Just because you are all guaranteed a job on graduation, it doesn't mean you should take it too easy,' Mr Cai, our supervisor in political studies, would sometimes say to students who he thought played too much and worked too little. There was indeed a small group of students who seemed to have rather indulged themselves in their new-found freedom after leaving home for the first time. They appeared to be quite relaxed and just did the bare minimum to pass their exams, secure in the knowledge that all of us would be assigned guaranteed jobs on graduation. In general, though, the campus life was filled with a good balance of hunger for knowledge and an appetite for fun, usually well blended together.

Meiling's arrival in the capital at the beginning of my second year changed my focus on the campus life, and I started to explore Beijing, which I had not really done to any great extent in the first year. My success in winning a university place in Beijing had encouraged Meiling to try to do the same in the entrance exam the following year.

Having come through triumphantly, Meiling now became a much-envied medical student in a key medical university in Beijing. There was so much for us to catch up with, and so much for us to explore together in the city that had excited both of us during our first visit some years ago. We traced the route we had taken during our first visit, and revisited the White Pagoda in Beihai Park. Walking down the *hutong* and tasting once again the city's famous *tanghulu*, the sugar-glazed hawthorn fruits, was also a delicious experience. We visited the Forbidden City, and savoured its magnificent architecture, its rich history and its superb collection of art. It soon became one of our favourite haunts, and every visit always seemed to bring new discoveries. Walking around the Summer Palace was also a brilliant experience, and its beautiful bridges and lake together with its innate tranquillity never failed to impress us.

Meiling had recently started having her meals in the 'small canteen' on her campus, the canteen catering specially for *Huis*, or Chinese Muslim lecturers and students in her university. Not that she had become a convert, she went there because of the food. It was not easy for Meiling to be allowed to dine there, and because of its size, the canteen was, generally speaking, not open to non-*Huis*. Wei, a third-year student from Huhehot, our home city, got her in, and he did it, I think, to impress her. As an active committee member of the student union, he certainly had some clout and was good at pulling strings. I remember him talking vividly, during one of my many visits to Meiling's university, about how he used to influence his boss when he worked in a pharmaceutical firm in Huhehot before he entered the university. Wei, also one of the 'old' school leavers, often became quite animated whenever I asked him to expand on some of his stories, which he relished telling. His small and engaging eyes moved fast behind his big glasses whenever he told us stories. 'Of course, you wouldn't know, because you're too young,' he would sometimes say to me, with the authority of somebody almost ten years older. To be fair to him, apart from being keen to show off, he was sympathetic to Meiling who had had a diet of steamed bread, boiled eggs and pickles for some time now. It wasn't that she didn't like cooked meals and vegetables, she simply didn't like the taste of lard, which the chefs at the 'big canteen', the canteen open to all the students in her university, seemed to have developed an over-reliance on. I still have a distinct memory of this canteen on her campus and the taste of the lard. One Saturday I went to visit Meiling on her campus, which I did often. Always keen to give me a treat, she splashed out and bought a portion of ribbon fish and some vegetables. As we were at the end of a long queue, by the time we got the food, it was pretty cold. 'Sorry, not as good as your ants climbing trees,' Meiling said apologetically, looking at the white layer of fat forming around the cooked cabbage. It was quite unpalatable, to say the least, and compared to her canteen food, the chefs in my university certainly did a much better job. It was not long after that Saturday that Meiling moved to the *Hui* canteen.

My memory of Meiling's campus was not all about the lard. The laboratory where she did experiments in Chinese herbal medicine, her speciality, was a fascinating place, with glass bottles of all shapes and sizes intricately connected to each other. I recall visiting her when she worked with a small group of fellow students on a feasibility study on producing herbal medicine in capsule form, a challenging task. With traditional herbal medicine, it is usually quite time-consuming to prepare and to decoct, that is, to boil and extract the substance of all the herb ingredients. There were already pre-decocted medicines available, but having herbal medicine in capsule form would be a convenient and much-welcomed solution. 'A great leap forward, little sister, as you'll see when you grow up,' Shenglong, a thin, bright 18-year-old with a quiet sense of humour in Meiling's group, liked to tease me whenever I went to visit Meiling at their laboratory. 'You'd better be right, big boss,' I often teased him in return, since he often talked about his ambition to become a leader of a large pharmaceutical company.

Peking duck tasted simply divine. I sat in a famous Peking duck restaurant for the first time with Meiling and Yang, the inspiring artist and Meiling's art teacher from our home city. Now studying in the top art academy in Beijing, he had just received a handsome payment, at least by student standards, from a magazine that had printed one of his works. I watched, with interest, a chef deftly turning a duck, attached to the end of a long pole, over an open fire that emitted a fragrance of burning apple wood and pear wood. 'That's our traditional way of cooking,' a young waitress proudly explained as she poured chrysanthemum tea for us. She then explained to us that all the ducks, often no more than 90 days old and no more than three kilos in weight, were all prepared and roasted following an old recipe which had made the restaurant famous since it was founded over a hundred years ago. Our duck arrived at our table in its beautiful Chinese red-date colour emitting tantalising fragrances. A young chef, in a white uniform and tall chef's hat, set to carve the duck for us. He first sliced the crispy skin and then placed the slices neatly on an oval plate. Then he set to slice the breasts, with each piece skilfully cut to the size of a lilac leaf and carefully placed on the plate. Finally, when the carving was completed, he broke the duck head into two and placed one half on each side of the plate of sliced duck meat.

With a pair of chopsticks, I took a couple of crispy duck pieces and dipped them in *tianmianjiang*, a sweet sauce similar to plum sauce in taste, then put them on to a lotus pancake, a small wafer-thin steamed pancake, before adding a few thinly-cut cucumber sticks and strips of spring onion. I then folded the lotus pancake into a small parcel and took my first bite. It was divine – the fragrance, the texture and the taste were all wonderful. For my second pancake parcel, I dipped a few duck pieces into soy sauce, then added ground garlic, cucumber and spring onion slices; that was equally delicious. Meiling and Yang were also delighted with the Peking duck, and, together, we savoured a piece of the culinary heritage of this ancient capital of culture.

University life in Beijing seemed to take on a fast pace, with much to do and a lot to explore, quite a contrast to life in our neighbourhood back home. Once I started at university, I would go home just twice a year, during the Spring Festival holiday and for the summer holiday. In between, I would write to my mother, who still didn't have a phone at home, though the frequency of my letters reduced as I became more and more involved with campus life and life in Beijing generally. Mother wrote to me more often and her letters would invariably bring some news of our neighbours. Madam Jiao, my mother wrote regretfully, had moved back to Taiyuan where she had come from, with her amiable husband Mr Wang and their adopted daughter Yaya.

Now that Meiling had left home as well, our small house had become quite empty, mostly occupied by just my mother and Yan, who, after failing to get a university place after three attempts, decided to abandon the idea of studying and resolved instead to concentrate on working her way up at the railway station, where she had now become the station's announcement broadcaster. At weekends my mother and Yan were often joined by Jing, who would return from a nearby city where she had been assigned to teach in a middle school after graduating from the polytechnic. With more time to herself, my mother pursued her interests in painting and botany. I was always quite impressed by her still-life watercolours when I saw them during the holidays. Madam Guan of course often came around to catch up with all the news. When I returned home for the holidays, I was struck by how she had aged since I had left home. The years of bringing up eight children seemed finally to have taken their toll on her, and her health had started to deteriorate, not helped by her constant smoking. She started to sigh a lot and to become a little despondent, particularly when talking about No. 7 and No. 8, who were both still waiting for employment after failing in the university entrance exam.

One of the highlights of university life for me was being a student tour guide in Guilin, a popular tourist city in south China. It was quite a common practice in the early 1980s for universities to organise their students in the third or fourth years to go out of campus and acquire some practical experience. In the same way as Meiling enjoyed her field trip gathering herbs in the mountains near Nanjing, I relished my three weeks in Guilin, taking in the breathtaking landscapes and practising my spoken English.

'Oh, look at those poor cormorants,' Jennifer, a slim, thirty-something American actress said, in a dramatic tone, looking at farmers on their flat, narrow rafts fishing with their cormorants on the Li River. I was with a group of American tourists, one of my first solo assignments. It was a hot summer's day, and watching the water buffalo cooling in the river and local children swimming downstream against the backdrop of the beautiful hills was tantalising. The tranquillity on the boat was somewhat broken by Jennifer's exclamation and soon my group's attention switched to me for an answer, or possibly even a justification. 'The cormorants are the pride and joy of the fishermen,' I argued, but my argument didn't satisfy Jennifer at all. She challenged me, again in a rather theatrical voice, how it could be OK for the 'lovely' cormorants to be tethered with the rings round the base of their necks and made to disgorge the fish after catching them. It was not an easy question to answer, and I started to struggle. Suddenly, I remembered the hard-working donkeys and mules in my home city. 'I think it is fine for the cormorants to do that for the fishermen, just as long as they are looked after well.' My explanation seemed to satisfy the group, most of whom nodded and went on enjoying our cruise on the river. Thinking about it now, some of them might have just agreed with me simply to stop Jennifer, famous for dramatising events – or picking bones from eggs, as Madam Guan would say. Suffice to say that my comprehension and speaking had progressed in leaps and bounds thanks to such questions, as well as the numerous and varied requests, not to forget the rather good collective sense of humour of the tourists.

'Why on earth do you have to wear glasses in interpreting class?' Mr Liu, a tall, square-jawed man in his fifties said to me one day in BBC English, having just summoned me to approach the podium during the break. An editor for a major English-language magazine in Beijing, he was a part-time lecturer who came to us once a week and whose lectures I loved. An inspiring man with an amazing depth of knowledge, a fantastic sense of humour and extremely high standards, he made interpreting challenging and sexy. 'So I can hear better,'

I replied while taking off my big heavy dark glasses, the sort of glasses most people were wearing at the time. I wasn't joking – it really seemed that I could hear better with my glasses on, even though it was probably purely psychological. 'Nonsense, I haven't heard anything so ridiculous in all my life,' he continued in English, which he liked to use to his favourite students. Then in a more avuncular way, he added, 'You don't look good in your glasses.'

But glasses were not the only thing which didn't look so good. With the fourth and final year arriving, apart from concentrating on exams and my dissertation, I started to become preoccupied about my future direction. A constant topic of conversation among classmates and friends now was about where we were likely to be assigned to after graduation. The consensus was that we, as graduates from a key university, would all get good assignments. After all, some of my well-informed friends insisted, government departments and offices, universities and research institutes in Beijing and other cities would take on a lot of fresh graduates, as they were in desperate need of fresh blood to fill the void created by the years of the Cultural Revolution.

'It is not fair that most students from the border and less-developed areas have to return to where they came from,' Zuo, who also came from Inner Mongolia, argued one day when we were all queuing for lunch. Then the usual debate went on, with some people in favour of the policy and some against. 'It's easy for you to take the high moral ground,' Zuo attacked Cheng, the Beijinger who said that graduates from the less-developed areas had a duty to serve the areas they came from. 'Don't tell me you are happy for your girlfriend to be assigned back to Xian,' Zuo said, with some disdain, to Cheng who was silenced.

With no time to lose, I quickly grabbed my lunch bowl and went straight to Mr Cai, our supervisor and a member of the university graduates assignment committee, to find out more about what I hoped was just a rumour. Since I had first heard about it a couple of weeks earlier, I had largely treated the 'news' as yet another piece of speculation from a small group of so-called well-informed people, who were not unknown for getting the wrong end of the stick. The debate in the canteen had somehow made me feel very nervous.

Mr Cai, a big, serious-looking man in his early thirties, looked quite surprised as he opened his door to me when I got to his third-floor flat in a purpose-built block for the university staff. I had never been to his flat before, and in fact, I had not heard of anybody who had. 'Any problem?' he asked in his serious, no-nonsense manner, as he put on his big dark glasses. I explained to him what I had heard and asked him to tell me whether it was true or not. He paused a little before offering me a seat in his sitting room piled with books and newspapers, very much a bachelor's pad. 'It is the policy set by the education ministry,' he confirmed. My white-enamelled bowl, filled with now cold lunch, was shaking in my hand as I tried to ask him to explain more, but there was not a lot to explain. 'A policy is a policy, and we have to follow it,' he continued, looking serious as ever.

My dream of living and working in Beijing, the city where I had left my heart behind during the visit to my grandfather some years before, was now in jeopardy. Having worked so hard to come here to study, I was determined to try my best to persuade Mr Cai to help me. Apart from my good academic results, I told him that I deserved to be given the chance to choose between Beijing and Inner Mongolia. 'My parents have done their bit by leaving the big city behind to support the development of Inner Mongolia, now it should be somebody else's turn,' I tried to convince Mr Cai.

My persuasion didn't seem to work, and Mr Cai repeated, matter-of-factly, that the committee had to stick by the policy set by the government. Things didn't look good for me, and I left his flat feeling pretty low, but I was determined not to give up trying. In the next month or so, I became a frequent visitor to Mr Cai's flat, often during lunch breaks or at supper time, when he seemed to have more time to listen. As we got to know each other better, between my persuasion and his mantra, we started to talk about Chinese literature, which he had specialised in as a worker-peasant-soldier student some years ago. 'You've got a good point there, but I cannot single-handedly change the policy,' he said one day. I was really pleased to hear that, because I could tell from his voice, which had gradually lost its severity, that he now wanted to help me. He didn't promise anything, but he said that he would make a case in my favour based on my argument, which he now believed made sense.

With Mr Cai on my side and with only two months to go before the 'big day' when we would know our destiny, I felt quietly optimistic that I would be among the small quota of students from the border areas not to be sent back. Then things took a bad turn, when Mr Cai brought me the news one day that one committee member, Madam Tan, our translation tutor, was opposed to me staying in Beijing. She was strongly in favour of the quota going to another person, and insisted that I lacked the gravitas to be a lecturer because I was too small and would be too young to work in a government ministry. I was flabbergasted that my size and age were raised as an issue, particularly from somebody who was known as Madam Penguin among our students because of her ungainly waddling and shuffling gait and her short, round body. 'What does size have to do with teaching?' I said to Mr Cai, quite incensed, resisting the temptation to make a personal attack on Madam Penguin. 'Has she not heard of Professor Su Buqing?' I mentioned the name of a very famous mathematician who was also a rather small man. I was passionate, and Mr Cai looked rather impressed with me for coming up with this example. Thinking about it, I still cannot remember where I had read about Professor Su's height, but the mere mention of the famous, diminutive professor with his towering talent seemed to work wonders for my case.

I was delighted when the news eventually came through that I had been assigned a job teaching at a university in Beijing. Obviously, Madam Penguin had only been trying to stitch me up so that she could help somebody else, somebody with *guanxi*, to get a job assignment in Beijing. Fortunately, Mr Cai and another member on the committee made a strong case in my favour based on my excellent academic record. Amid many parties and some tears, my classmates and I said our goodbyes after four years together. Min and Lei were both very pleased to return to Shanghai for jobs in government offices. Zuo, the philosopher, returned to Inner Mongolia, while Qian, who would otherwise have been assigned back to Xian, got a research job in Beijing to be together with Cheng, originally from the capital, now that they were engaged.

It was a beautiful summer, a summer filled with anticipation and hope. I started to look forward to sharing with others my knowledge of English, the subject I had loved since a young age, and hoped that I could be as inspiring as Teacher Zhang and Miss Liang. Four years in university had, however, broadened my horizons, and there was now so much else I also wanted to do. I wanted to travel and to see the world, the wider world which my English had, in my mind, already taken me to. I wanted to run a small art gallery, now that I enjoyed the world of art, thanks to the introduction of Meiling and Yang. My dream of becoming a writer also beckoned. And so, with all these possibilities in front of me, with the optimism of youth and as a fresh graduate at the age of 19, I felt the world was my oyster and was thrilled to live in a city full of opportunity and promise.

Epilogue

It was a beautiful autumn morning. Drizzle overnight had brought a freshness to the air, and early risers were already into their morning exercise routines in Chaoyang Park in east Beijing. Runners, mostly young or middle-aged, ran with their state-of-the-art mobiles and iPods either hanging around their necks or clipped on to their trendy sportswear. Enthusiasts of *taiji* gathered in groups and were immersed in this traditional Chinese exercise, now much back in vogue. The enthusiasts, mostly old people but with a few young faces, concentrated on slow motions to feel their *qi*, a vital internal energy. There were quite a few walkers around, with some walking backwards, as this was considered by some locals to be good for balance and muscle tone.

Beijing in 2007 was a vibrant city full of optimism and anticipation. As the host city to the 2008 Olympic Games, the city was busy with preparations for the big day. Gardeners were planting flowers and shrubs next to the recently widened and newly named Olympic View Boulevard leading to Chaoyang Park, one of the venues for the Games.

I had come to the park that morning to watch my mother do her *taiji*. She had been doing this for months now and, every morning, almost without fail, she would come here at seven to join her group. Soon to be 80, my mother looked remarkably well – she had clearly been enjoying living in Beijing since she moved here some 16 years ago – and watching her manoeuvring her flexible sword, with some considerable skill and agility, was a real treat and a precious experience for me, now that I lived in England.

'Fancy you still speaking such good Chinese!' Madam Li, one of my mother's *taiji* friends, exclaimed after the exercises, while her husband proudly and lovingly stroked their white Pekingese. The dog, well groomed and well attired in a Burberry-style check jacket, looked contented and occasionally barked, a bit half-heartedly, at passers-by. Pet ownership was a relatively new trend in Beijing, and it would have been unthinkable, when I was a young girl, to have had a pet dog. We simply could not have afforded to feed a dog, nor did we have enough space for one.

I gave Madam Li one of my polite smiles, yet her compliment, though well-intentioned, made me feel a little uneasy and filled me with some considerable doubts about my command of Chinese. 'Of course your Chinese is good, it's your mother tongue,' my mother tried to console me, having detected my doubts. 'Besides, being here for a month will really help to keep it fluent,' my mother added with a smile, and she was right. My regular visits back, and the interim years of living in China during my husband Peter's period of working here, have helped a great deal to keep my colloquial Chinese up to date. Yet the truth of the matter is that, having lived in England for nearly twenty years, my spoken Chinese is not as fluent as it should be, and this is particularly noticeable in food shopping. Time has played a trick on me and also, over the past two decades, China has gone through dramatic changes. With so many cuts of pork, beef and lamb to choose from, my earlier shopping experiences, which had mostly just stretched to buying offal during rationing, no longer gave me the right vocabulary.

The supermarket near Chaoyang Park was busy with shoppers, with some whizzing around and some seemingly enjoying window shopping, or shelf shopping in this case. There were indeed many things on offer, from hi-fi equipment to sewing kits, and from Chinese pickles to imported biscuits. The dairy section in particular had attracted many people, apparently prompted by the popular calcium awareness campaigns in the media, who were carefully choosing from a large selection of different types of milk and yogurt. 'Remember them?' my mother said with a touch of nostalgia, as she picked up a couple of vacuum-packed bags of milk with pictures of Friesian cows grazing on the Mongolian steppes printed on them. I nodded, and the mention of the Friesians took me right back to the river-bank where Mr Ma's cows had grazed and to the dairy where my mother used to take me for my treat of fresh milk. I can still smell the aroma of the heated milk and taste the layer of cream floating deliciously in the small china bowl. I wanted to tell my mother how ashamed I often felt now whenever I thought about how relieved I had been, as a child, when she had turned down my offer of a sip of my precious milk. But I didn't, because I didn't know how to, not without bringing tears to her eyes. Lately, as my mother has aged, I have noticed that she has become more nostalgic and sentimental.

The butcher's counter in the supermarket also attracted a large crowd, and chicken wings and legs were quickly disappearing, while pork and beef were also shifting fast. 'Remember the offal shop and the fortune-teller with the big glasses?' I said to my mother as we were choosing a piece of pork leg. 'He would have had a field day here,' my mother said with a hearty laugh. With the piece of pork leg, I was all set to cook a roast pork supper in the brand-new oven at Meiling's plush apartment. Ovens are a relatively new item that are gradually being introduced to Chinese kitchens, especially in new apartments. 'I'd better pull out all the stops,' I said to my mother, as I had earlier promised Meiling's 12-year-old son Tongtong, who had been much entertained by my story of being chased by some barking Gloucester Old Spot piglets on a Gloucestershire farm, that my roast pork was something worth waiting for, and I was keen to make his first experience of a home-cooked 'western' meal a memorable one.

My own first experience of a home-cooked Sunday lunch was on an autumn day in 1989 in the beautiful Sussex home of Melody, a warm, kind and generous friend who, together with Ernest, another friend, had sponsored my visit to the UK. 'Yorkshire pudding?' I repeated, a little baffled. I remember that I searched deep in my vocabulary and struggled to understand why Yorkshire pudding, which my logic told me must be a dessert, should be offered with the main course. A little too shy to ask, I turned it down, to the surprise of Melody who knew that I loved food. It didn't take long for her to work out the reason for my confusion and soon afterwards I was persuaded into trying both the Yorkshire pudding and subsequently the real dessert, a chocolate roulade, her signature dish. Having Sunday lunch with her family and friends not only tested my spoken English but also my ability to handle a knife and fork. Although knives and forks were not totally foreign to me – I had used them occasionally in western-style restaurants in China during my spell as a tour guide – relying on them fully and in the company of experts was, nevertheless, a daunting prospect, to say the least. Cutting the roast potatoes was easy and I was quite pleased with myself to start with, I recall, for not letting the side down. My confidence soon started to recede, however, as I ventured on to my beef. It was not so easy and I struggled. As usual, help was at hand, and Melody had found me a teacher in Michael who was sitting next to me. There was a glitch, though, as Michael is left-handed, and it took him a little while to work out that perhaps he should swap his knife and fork around for the demonstration. His tips seemed to help, until the second piece I cut flew off my plate and landed, embarrassingly, on the well-ironed white linen tablecloth.

It is quite amusing now to think that my embarrassment of losing control of the flying beef featured so prominently in my memories of that lunch. It seems, to some extent, that it has overshadowed everything else. Thinking about it now, I cannot really remember much of the taste of that lunch, except that it looked impressive, plentiful and very different. In a way, I suppose that my palate, much more used to highly flavoured and spicy Chinese food at that time, must have found English food a little bland and less varied. It didn't take long, though, for me to start enjoying Melody's delicious home cooking. In fact, I was quick to put her tips into practice when my friend Dr Shan came to visit me on the Gloucestershire farm where I then lived, and the farm which was, some years later, made famous by Stinking Bishop cheese and its association with Wallace and Gromit.

I had met Shan through a friend of a friend in the early 1990s when he was studying at Imperial College in London. He was one of the *crème de la crème*, one of a small group of graduates that had been chosen to study abroad on a Chinese government grant. A good cook, Shan often entertained me with Chinese food whenever I went to visit him in London. His repertoire included chicken wings and drumsticks, Chinese cabbage, and spare ribs in dark sauce. Like most people from south China, Shan was particularly fond of rice, and his *Yangzhou* fried rice was quite an exceptional dish. With this dish, Shan would first beat a couple of eggs, cook them in heated oil, and wait until the egg mixture expanded into a golden yellow 'pancake'. He would then shake the frying pan a little before tossing the pancake in the air. When it was cooked, he would then transfer it on to a chopping board. In the meantime, he would heat some more oil in a wok and then, into the hot oil, he would add cubed ham, peas and chopped prawns before giving all this a good mix and stir. He would then add boiled rice, cucumber cubes and the fried eggs now chopped into small squares. Another mix and stir, a little seasoning with salt, and a simple but delicious dish was ready to be served. Sometimes, if I was lucky, I could even lay my hands on some Eight Treasures, my favourite pickle from Beijing's famous *Liubiju*, which I had first been introduced to by my cousins' friends many years ago. A popular gathering place, Shan's small flat, shared with a few other Chinese students, became something of a centre for home food brought over both by newcomers and by people who had just returned from visiting China.

Shan had not had very much English food, and it seemed to be the norm among overseas Chinese to stick mostly to Chinese food. So with the food on the farm, I wanted to give him a taste of English cooking. I set out to prepare him a traditional English roast meal. Having selected a nice leg of pork – from one of the Gloucester Old Spot pigs raised on the farm, I rinsed the pork under the cold tap and then dried it thoroughly with a piece of kitchen towel. With a Stanley knife in hand, I scored the skin and then rubbed some rock salt and milk over it before I put it into the oven. I then briefly boiled some potatoes and parsnips, peeled and cut into halves, before I put them in a tray, preheated with vegetable oil, adding a few cloves of garlic, one of my favourite ingredients. The apple sauce was made of Transparent, a fragrant cooking apple and an old Gloucestershire variety. For the gravy, I used some of the meat juice from the roasting tray and added flour, an Oxo cube, some home-grown herbs and finally my 'secret weapon', a spoonful of damson jam made with fruit from the farm. Seasoned with a little salt and pepper, the gravy was a great accompaniment to the tender and flavoursome pork. Shan particularly liked the crackling and, enhanced by the salt and milk, I also had to admit that it was quite exceptional. I remember that I was really pleased with the outcome, as cooking like this was in fact quite new to me. Before I came to England, I had never seen an oven, let alone used one.

Entertained by my stories of England, Meiling's son, to my relief, also much enjoyed my roast. His first experience of the home-cooked crackling, apple sauce and gravy was so favourable that he asked me to show Meiling exactly how to do it, so that he could have it more often. As an only child, Tongtong is a much-indulged, though not spoilt, child, and he is particularly indulged by my mother who now lives with Meiling's family. It is interesting just to observe the lengths to which my mother goes in order to make a meal that he enjoys. Thinking about it, my mother has always been like this, except that when we were young, she was simply not able to do so.

'What treasure do you have there, Grandma?' Tongtong was in a teasing mood as my mother called me over to the dining table where she brought over a small parcel neatly wrapped in a piece of red paper. She unfolded the wrapping, carefully and slowly, as if she were unveiling a fragile antique. 'I have always meant to tell you, but have always felt too guilty to do so,' she signed, with tears in her eyes. I didn't know what to expect and indeed what to say. There, in front of my eyes, were the five pig toes from my childhood game, all well-cleaned and mani-cured. 'Grandma, why toes?' Tongtong asked, his voice filled with curiosity. Then my mother told the story of how she had hidden the pig toes which my friend Fei had given me. 'They didn't just disappear, as I told you, they were always on the window sill in the kitchen,' mother sighed, her voice full of guilt, sorrow and regret.

Now that my mother mentioned the episode, I remember that I had been quite upset and annoyed with myself for losing the pig toes, but my annoyance was transient, and I recall that I soon moved on from the pig-toe game. Mother's story now also reminded me of her uncharacteristic lack of response when I told her about the mysterious disappearance of my pig toes, which I remember I didn't quite understand at that time. 'Mama, it's nothing, and I wasn't very good at the game anyway,' I tried to make light of something that had happened over thirty years ago. 'That's why you were not very good, because I deprived you of the chance to get better, poor child,' she sighed again. I looked at her. Her silver hair frames her face, weathered with the advance of the years, and her almond eyes, as beautiful as ever, are filled with tenderness and kindness.

It seems that my mother's guilt about hiding my pig toes has been compounded by an article she has recently come across. According to the author, an educationalist, games such as the pig-toe game are precious to children and also extremely good for the development of children's dexterity and intelligence. Not only did she feel bad for having hidden the toes and for having subsequently misled me, but she also felt that she had deprived me of something precious to a child. My mother is really a little hard on herself, and, looking back, she simply did what she thought was the best for me at that time. She had many reasons to do so. After all, the pig-toe game was quite addictive and many girls in our neighbourhood were so absorbed in it that their studies suffered. At a time when even optimists had to struggle to see the bright side, my mother felt that the only way for us to have any chance in life was to study hard and to excel. It was a tumultuous time, a time when it was difficult to spot any opportunities in life, because there were rarely any, not for us anyway.

'Oh, well, so you've kept them for over thirty years then?' Tongtong asked. As intelligent as he is, it was inevitably difficult for him to fully understand that irrational time that Meiling and the rest of us had grown up in. 'I wish I had,' my mother said, explaining that the original toes had been lost somewhere. Then, lightening up a little, she added, 'they were better polished and painted red.' 'You'd better paint them red then, little sister,' Tongtong, a product of a happy time, said to me, cheerfully and a little mischievously, before going to his room to carry on with his homework.

It is the National Day holiday again, a major week-long holiday in China. Amid the chopping, the chatting and the clattering of pans and woks, Jing is in her element cooking in Meiling's large kitchen where we are preparing a birthday lunch for my mother. We are also celebrating the success of Meiling's first exhibition of her own work recently held at the National Museum of China. Meiling is now an established professional artist and has a lot to celebrate, having just exhibited over one hundred oil paintings in the National Museum on the east side of the famous square, the square she frequently painted on our school posters many years ago. Jing has come to Beijing from Huhehot, our home city, where she now teaches in No. 2 Middle School. Like No. 1 Middle School, my alma mater, and the rest of the schools in Huhehot, her school is no longer affiliated to the railway bureau but is now under the control of the municipal government. As a result of many years of the one-child policy, both her school and No. 1 have to be proactive in recruiting pupils to fill their places – so different to when I had to fight for my middle-school place many years ago. With me living in the UK, Jing in Huhehot and the others in Beijing, it is not that often now that we four sisters and our mother gather together, so our condensed time together is invariably filled with a lot of chatting and reminiscing. It sometimes makes me smile to think that I used to laugh at Madam Guan and my mother for talking about their past. I thought then, as a child, that reminiscing was the preserve of old people. As the only one of my family who still lives in our home city, Jing has become our only source of news from there. Teacher Zhang, now retired from full-time work, teaches part-time in one of the city's private schools, where Miss Liang also teaches part-time. Our neighbourhood has long disintegrated, with the Guans and Mr Ma's family being the last ones to leave, and there are no longer any Friesian cows on the riverbank. As part of a regeneration project, our row of terraced houses and all the other houses in our neighbourhood have been demolished, and, instead, blocks of five-storey buildings now stand in their places. 'Guan Jie phoned me the other day, and he wanted a few tips on learning English,' Jing tells us, and the mention of Guan No. 8 reminds me of the mischievous boy on his eighth birthday. That birthday, over thirty years ago, seems like yesterday, and I can almost hear Madam Guan, who is now no longer with us, scolding the 'naughty No. 8'. Like all his siblings, No. 8 still lives in our home city, and he has just recently started a taxi business. 'He hopes learning English will help his business as more foreign tourists are coming to China now,' Jing explains. I admire No. 8 for starting to learn English in his forties, and in fact, I have recently noticed quite a few Beijing taxi drivers working hard at their English for the Beijing Olympics.

Yan does what she does best. With the fresh fruits and vegetables she has just bought, she is preparing some large juicy tomatoes, a far cry from the small, green tomatoes she used to bring home after hours of queuing many years ago. Yan now works as a statistician in a railway company near Beijing, and she is very lucky to have found this well-paid contract work after she lost the 'iron rice bowl' several years ago. The iron rice bowl she inherited from my mother by succeeding her at the railway station in our home city proved to be less solid than she believed when she first started in her 'job for life'. Having worked her way up from a ticket conductor at the railway station to a statistician with the help of an open university degree, she now needs to adjust to a life as a contract worker, in which she has to think about her own pension and health insurance, both of which the old iron rice bowl system used to take care of automatically.

The star anise wafts through from a pot of beef coming from the steppes of Inner Mongolia, and toasted chilli, spring onion, ginger, garlic and fresh coriander are sending out mouthwatering fragrances. I have been tasked to cook *chaomian*, or fried noodles. *Chaomian*, or *chowmein* as it is also known, is an easy and tasty dish to do, and since noodles carry a connotation of longevity, it is a good dish to have for our mother's eightieth birthday. I cook *chaomian* often. Into a wok with heated oil, I would add finely chopped spring onion until the fragrance appears, before adding shredded pork. I would then stir-fry the meat until cooked, then add chilli sauce, soy sauce, salt and a little rice wine. Then I add lettuce, cut into thin strips, and freshly boiled home-made noodles, mix thoroughly and stir-fry until it is cooked.

The sweet and sour king prawns taste exceptional, and the beef is tender and packed with flavours. Amid much talking and laughter, we are enjoying a feast with our extended families. There is *mapo doufu*, a hot and spicy bean curd and *yuxiang rousi* cooked with shredded pork, red chillies, bamboo shoots and *muer*, a dark Chinese fungus. There is Chinese long leaf cooked with *gouqi* berries and fried runner beans with Chinese mushrooms, and of course, lion's head and four happiness. For old times' sake, we have even prepared some *songhua* eggs to accompany *jiaozi*, the delicious dumplings. The sweetcorn buns with dates, which we often used to have during rationing many years ago, are also very popular. Sweetcorn buns, together with millet and many other things we loved to hate during rationing, have once again entered the Chinese diet, but they are now prized for their health-bestowing characteristics and so are expensive. To make the lunch even more of a feast, Meiling has had a Peking duck delivered with all the sauces and the lotus pancakes. With French red wine sent by some friends, we toast our mother, the birthday girl. Mother is, as usual, busy making sure everybody else has plenty, as she used to do when I was young, even though we now have an abundance of food spread across the large dining table. She is at her happiest when she is looking after others, and it is no different even though today is her day.

Chaomian proves to be quite a success. As I watch everybody tucking in, I think of the noodles Madam Guan cooked after my father's funeral so many years ago, and it all flashes back to me. 'Eat some for your father's sake,' the words of Madam Jiao, another old neighbour, ring in my ears. She meant that Meiling and I should eat the noodles for my father's longevity in the next life. I hoped the noodles had worked. If so, my father would be able to see my mother's birthday celebration from his place in heaven. I am sure he would be smiling at us indulgently and would have approved it all.

Glossary

ants climbing trees: minced pork in mung-bean vermicelli

baijiu: 'white alcohol', strong colourless liquor distilled from sorghum and other grain

chilema: greeting used in the author's hometown of Huhehot (literally 'Have you eaten?')

chaomian: also known as 'chow mein', fried noodles

duilian: scroll bearing good luck/health/happiness message

erhu: two-stringed bowed musical instrument

four happiness: small meatballs, usually made with pork

fu: good fortune

gouqi berries: red berries of *Lycium barbarum*; hailed as a 'superfood'; known by various names in the UK, including goji, Chinese wolfberry, Chinese boxthorn, red medlar

guanxi: social and business connections, often used to obtain favours, promotion, etc.

Han: the largest ethnic group in the People's Republic of China, comprising about 90 per cent of the population

Hui: a Chinese ethnic group, Muslim Chinese

hutong: ancient narrow alley

iron rice bowl: a job for life, guaranteed lifetime employment in state enterprises

jiaozi: small dumplings, favoured as a festival food

jineijin: cooked chicken's stomach membrane

kang: heated brick bed

lao: old, as a friendly prefix (as in 'old chap')

Laobing: Chinese pancake

liang: weight measurement, approximately 50 grams

lion's head: large meatball shaped to resemble a lion's head

Longjing: a type of green tea

mahua: deep-fried sweet dough twist with sesame seeds

mairujing: malted milk drink

mapo dufu: hot spicy dish of bean curd and minced meat, usually pork or beef

matang: a kind of sweet

muer: a type of edible fungus

nihao: informal greeting

ninhao: formal greeting

Putonghua: standard spoken form of the Chinese language, based on the Beijing dialect

qi: inner energy

Qingming: Tomb-Sweeping Day, a festival of remembrance, which normally falls on or around 5 April

songhua eggs: normally duck eggs, hard boiled and preserved in a mixture of lime and salt, also known as hundred-year-old or thousand-year-old eggs

tanghulu: 'sugar gourds', sugar-glazed hawthorn fruits

taiji: tai chi, a traditional Chinese exercise famous for its slow and controlled movements, promoting well-being, fitness and vitality

worker-peasant-soldier student: student with work experience, chosen from all walks of life and admitted to university during the years of the Cultural Revolution. The selection was mostly based on the student's achievements at work and recommendations from his or her superiors, rather than the result of entrance exams

yuxiang rousi: 'fish-flavoured' sliced pork dish

zongzi: pyramid-shaped parcels of glutinous rice and other sweet and/or savoury fillings in bamboo or reed leaves

Acknowledgements

The book is not just my story of growing up in China, it is also about the celebration of food. It often amazes me how prominently food features in my childhood memories, and I hope that my account has done justice to all the delicious and memorable food my mother and sisters cooked with enormous creativity and based on very limited supplies. Thanking them publicly will probably embarrass them, but I still want to do so, both for giving me the inspiration and for helping me to remember while I was working on the book.

The constant interest from friends and family has also been a great source of encouragement, and I would particularly like to thank Melody Dack, Charles Martell and Yang Tianshuo for their enthusiasm and help in thinking about the title.

I would also like to thank the team at Vintage and Random House, in particular Rachel Cugnoni, Beth Coates and Alison Hennessey, who have touched me with their real enthusiasm and kind encouragement. I should like to add a special note of thanks to Alison as my editor, whose critical insights and excellent suggestions I have found invaluable. Vivien Green, my agent, deserves a big thank-you for having faith in me, and for being so professional and nice.

Finally, I would like to thank my husband Peter for everything. Not only has he put up with me disappearing into my own world from time to time while writing, but he also, brilliantly and often with good humour, has acted in the multiple role of critic, sounding board and adviser. Suffice it to say that this book would not have been possible without his constant support.

www.vintage-books.co.uk